It's a
Weird World

It's a
Weird World

Paul Stirling Hagerman

Illustrated by Myron Miller

 Sterling Publishing Co., Inc.   New York

Library of Congress Cataloging-in-Publication Data

Hagerman, Paul Stirling.
   It's a weird world / Paul Stirling Hagerman ; illustrated by Myron
Miller.
     p. cm.
   "Much of the material . . . compiled and excerpted from . . .
Hagerman's It's an odd world . . . and It's a mad mad world"—T.p.
verso.
   Includes index.
   Summary: A collection of humorous true anecdotes and odd facts
about the world, in such categories as "At the Movies," "Odd Jobs,"
and "What's in a Name."
   1. Curiosities and wonders—Juvenile literature.   [1. Curiosities
and wonders.]   I. Miller, Myron, 1948–   ill. II. Title.
AG243.H1986   1990
031.02—dc20   90-37643
                                                    CIP
                                                    AC

10 9 8 7 6 5 4 3 2 1

© 1990 by Sterling Publishing Company, Inc.
387 Park Avenue South, New York, N.Y. 10016
Portions of the material in this book appeared previously
in *It's an Odd World* and *It's a Mad Mad World* by Paul Stirling Hagerman
© 1977, 1978 by Sterling Publishing Company, Inc.
Distributed in Canada by Sterling Publishing
% Canadian Manda Group, P.O. Box 920, Station U
Toronto, Ontario, Canada M8Z 5P9
Distributed in Great Britain and Europe by Cassell PLC
Villiers House, 41/47 Strand, London WC2N 5JE, England
Distributed in Australia by Capricorn Ltd.
P.O. Box 665, Lane Cove, NSW 2066
Manufactured in the United States of America

Sterling   ISBN 0-8069-5412-5   Paper

With love to
Barbara Briggs Hagerman

CONTENTS

AND NOW FOR SOMETHING COMPLETELY DIFFERENT

◆1◆
HOW IT STARTED

The vending machine has been around since the time of Christ. The first vending machine was a coin-operated holy water dispenser invented by the Greek scientist, Hero, in the first century B.C.

◆   ◆   ◆   ◆   ◆

Experts believe that the counting-out rhyme, "Eena, Meena, Mina, Mo," used in games to select who is "It," may have originally come from an incantation used by ancient pagans in choosing human sacrifices.

◆ ◆ ◆ ◆ ◆

Geronimo, the famous Apache Indian chief, was not named Geronimo. His real name was Goyathlay, which means "one who yawns." Mexican settlers in the area referred to the fearless Indian chief as "Jerome," which in Spanish is "Geronimo."

One of the most famous incidents in Geronimo's life was a daring leap he made to escape the U.S. cavalry. He jumped from a high cliff into a river, supposedly shouting his name, "Geronimo!" as he fell. The incident was featured in a 1940 movie and inspired paratroopers during World War II to shout "Geronimo!" as they jumped.

◆ ◆ ◆ ◆ ◆

The term "love" in tennis is said to come from the French word "l'oeuf" meaning "egg" because a zero is egg-shaped. The sccring system (fifteen, thirty, forty, game) is believed to have been derived from the position of the hands on a clock face. The third point was originally called "forty-five."

◆ ◆ ◆ ◆ ◆

In December 1891 a physical-education instructor at the Y.M.C.A. Training School in Springfield, Massachusetts, invented a new game. He asked the school janitor to find two boxes and nail them at opposite ends of the gymnasium balcony. The janitor couldn't find any boxes so he substituted two peach baskets. If the janitor had been able to find some boxes, the game probably would have become known as "box-ball"; instead it was named "basketball."

◆ ◆ ◆ ◆ ◆

Nipper, the symbol of RCA Victor records, was based on an early 20th century painting entitled "His Master's Voice." An artist was listening to a recording of the voice of his brother who had recently died. Upon hearing the voice, his dead brother's dog immediately jumped up and cocked his ear towards the speaker. The artist depicted this incident in a painting that showed his brother's coffin, with the dog sitting on top listening to the Victrola. The scene (minus the coffin, of course) became the symbol of RCA Victor.

◆　◆　◆　◆　◆

Henri Charpentier, the famous chef of one of the Princes of Wales, accidentally invented Crepes Suzettes when the dessert he was making caught on fire. It was named for a young girl who witnessed the conflagration.

◆　◆　◆　◆　◆

Although the frankfurter is generally thought of as German, it was actually invented by the ancient Chinese.

◆　◆　◆　◆　◆

The pawnbroker's traditional symbol, three golden balls, was inspired by the three globes on the coat of arms of the Medicis, who were the richest money-lenders in Florence.

◆　◆　◆　◆　◆

Coffee-drinking first became popular in Europe after the siege of Vienna in 1683, when coffee beans and coffee-making equipment were left behind by the retreating Turks.

◆　◆　◆　◆　◆

The first man to breed mules in the United States was George Washington.

◆　◆　◆　◆　◆

Why do outhouse doors have crescent moons on them? Scholars who devote their lives to studying such things explain that early outhouses had either a crescent moon, a traditional symbol for things for use by women, or a sun, a traditional symbol for men. Since most people were illiterate, simply printing "Men" and "Women" on the doors was useless.

The women typically kept their outhouses neat, tidy, pleasant and in good repair. Men's outhouses, on the other hand, quickly degenerated into shambles and collapsed.

The difference in the survival rate of male and female outhouses was so great that over the years the crescent moon slowly became the universal symbol for all outhouses.

♦ ♦ ♦ ♦ ♦

It is said that Frederick the Great of Prussia ordered buttons to be sewn on the sleeves of army uniforms after he saw a soldier wiping his nose on his sleeve. The row of buttons prevented the soldiers from using their sleeves as makeshift handkerchiefs. The story may or may not be true, but nevertheless men's coats have had a row of otherwise useless buttons on the sleeve since the time of Frederick the Great.

♦ ♦ ♦ ♦ ♦

The dollar sign is a modification of the figure eight as it appeared on the old Spanish "pieces of eight."

♦ ♦ ♦ ♦ ♦

When we think of bagpipes, we invariably think of Scotland. However, the bagpipe is not uniquely Scottish, nor was it invented there. Various types of bagpipes are found in other countries. The instrument was introduced to Scotland by the Romans, and it probably is as old as the ancient Persian empire.

♦ ♦ ♦ ♦ ♦

The world's oldest folk song is probably "Drink to Me Only with Thine Eyes," with lyrics written by the third-century Greek poet Philostratus the Athenian. It was translated into English in 1616 by England's great dramatist, Ben Jonson.

◆ ◆ ◆ ◆ ◆

Sunglasses first became popular when movie stars began wearing them during the early days of filmmaking. The general public soon began wearing them too. Actually, early film actors wore sunglasses not because they wanted to look mysterious or romantic, but because their eyes hurt. The early movie lights designed by the Kliegl brothers were so intensely bright that they caused a painful affliction known as "kliegl eyes." Actors took to wearing sunglasses whenever possible so that they could give their eyes some rest.

◆ ◆ ◆ ◆ ◆

The ceremony of toasting comes from the custom of dropping a piece of toasted spiced bread into a glass of wine to improve its flavor. When we toast a person we are in effect saying that his presence adds flavor to the party. The custom of clinking glasses is an ancient practice whose original purpose was to scare off evil spirits so that they wouldn't enter the body through the liquor.

◆ ◆ ◆ ◆ ◆

Thomas Edison is responsible for the word "Hello" being a standard telephone greeting. When the first telephone exchange was installed in Connecticut in 1878, the company recommended that people answer their phones by loudly shouting, "Ahoy! Ahoy!" into the mouthpiece. Edison suggested the more subdued greeting "Hello" and the word caught on.

◆ ◆ ◆ ◆ ◆

The practice sentence used in typing, "Now is the time for all good men to come to the aid of their party," is as old as the typewriter itself. A court reporter coined the expression to test the efficiency of the first practical typewriter, constructed by his close friend Christopher Sholes.

♦   ♦   ♦   ♦   ♦

The huddle used in American football was invented at Gaulladet College, a university for the deaf in Washington, D.C., to prevent the opposing team from seeing their hand signals.

♦   ♦   ♦   ♦   ♦

All three of the most commonly-used artificial sweeteners of the 20th century were discovered by accident. Aspartame, also known as Nutri-Sweet, was discovered in 1965 by a chemist searching for a new ulcer drug. Cyclamate was discovered in 1937 when a researcher, working on developing a new fever-reducing drug, flicked some tobacco off his lips and wondered why his fingers tasted so sweet. Saccharin was discovered in 1879 by two university scientists investigating the medicinal properties of coal tar derivatives.

♦   ♦   ♦   ♦   ♦

The hood ornament on BMW automobiles doesn't have anything to do with automobiles. It's a stylized airplane propeller. BMW was originally an aircraft manufacturer, and when it stopped making planes and started making cars, it kept the old company symbol.

♦   ♦   ♦   ♦   ♦

The familiar lanky, Yankee, goateed figure of Uncle Sam was based on a circus clown character created by Dan Rice, a star clown of the 1840's.

♦   ♦   ♦   ♦   ♦

Velcro was invented in 1948 by a Swiss engineer, George deMestral, who came home from a walk in the woods one day, and was irritated to find cockleburrs stuck all over his clothes as well as his dog's coat. He decided to find out why they stuck so stubbornly without any adhesive substance.

Under the microscope he discovered that the burr's ends were actually tiny hooks that grabbed onto anything fuzzy. The hook-and-loop fastener was born. Its name was a combination of velvet and *crochet,* the French word for hook.

◆　◆　◆　◆　◆

While in prison in Minnesota in 1887, outlaw Jesse James and two of the Younger Boys contributed $50 to start a prison newspaper. The newspaper, *The Prison Mirror,* continues to this day and has won numerous journalism awards.

◆　◆　◆　◆　◆

The characteristic tail fins on the cars of the 1950s were inspired by automotive designer Harley Earl's fascination with the vertical stabilizers of the F-38 fighter plane.

◆　◆　◆　◆　◆

◆ 2 ◆

NOT STRANGER THAN FICTION

The type of diet that American people consider to be ideal will kill a monkey within a very short period of time.

◆　◆　◆　◆　◆

When a gorilla is angry, he will stick out his tongue at you.

◆　◆　◆　◆　◆

In Tibet, it is a sign of respect to stick out your tongue at guests.

Bird Talk

Flamingoes are only able to eat with their heads upside down.

♦ ♦ ♦ ♦ ♦

People who talk to their canaries are wasting their time (and the canary's). Canaries can hear only very high-pitched tones. Although a canary might respond to sound vibrations and your body movements, it can't hear a word you're saying (unless you have a voice like another canary).

♦ ♦ ♦ ♦ ♦

There are virtually no birds that sing while they are on the ground. Birds typically sing only when they are on a tree branch or on some other spot off the ground.

♦ ♦ ♦ ♦ ♦

The weight of a sparrow's brain makes up about 4.2% of its total body weight. Comparatively, man's brain is considerably smaller than that of a sparrow—only 2.5% of his total body weight.

♦ ♦ ♦ ♦ ♦

It takes about four hours to hard-boil an ostrich egg.

♦ ♦ ♦ ♦ ♦

More trained pigeons (over 56,000) were used as communications couriers in World War II than in any other war in history. Several were awarded medals for gallantry under fire.

Life in the U.S.

According to a world-wide medical study, Americans lead the world in headache suffering.

♦   ♦   ♦   ♦   ♦

According to a survey of sun-worshippers, the most popular participant sport in American nudist camps is volleyball.

♦   ♦   ♦   ♦   ♦

The United States Forest Service spent $60,000 on a research project devoted to the task of designing a better outhouse.

♦   ♦   ♦   ♦   ♦

It is illegal to hunt camels in Arizona.

♦   ♦   ♦   ♦   ♦

The famous gambling center, Las Vegas, claims to have the highest number of churches per capita in the entire world.

♦   ♦   ♦   ♦   ♦

A government study has discovered that residents of Nevada (where gambling is legal) gamble more than tourists do.

♦   ♦   ♦   ♦   ♦

According to the Nielsen television rating figures, the average American child views 18,000 television murders by the time he is 18 years old—in contrast to spending only 11,000 hours in school.

♦   ♦   ♦   ♦   ♦

California is the world's leading producer of prunes.

The site of the biblical sin city of Sodom is rapidly becoming a booming tourist area.

♦　♦　♦　♦　♦

The number of possible bridge hands a player might be dealt adds up to 635,013,559,599. It would be possible to deal one bridge hand every hour for over 72,000,000 years without getting the same hand.

♦　♦　♦　♦　♦

Studies have shown that raindrops are not raindrop-shaped. They are generally round or spheroid and some studies say they are sometimes doughnut-shaped.

♦　♦　♦　♦　♦

According to careful scientific measurement, almost 95 percent of an automobile's mechanical engine wear occurs in the first ten seconds after the cold engine is started. Also, the gas mileage of an engine in the first few minutes after starting is less than a third of that of a warm engine.

♦　♦　♦　♦　♦

Lightning strikes somewhere on earth about 6,000 times every minute. Fortunately, it generally strikes mountain tops and skyscrapers rather than homes and people. If it could be harnessed, a powerful lightning bolt could produce enough energy to lift a large ocean liner six feet into the air.

♦　♦　♦　♦　♦

Just before you are struck by lightning, all the hair on your head will stand on end.

♦　♦　♦　♦　♦

There are close to 2,000 thunderstorms going on around the world at this very moment.

♦　♦　♦　♦　♦

According to the scientific scale used to measure hardness, a shark's tooth is quite literally as hard as steel. When biting, a medium-sized shark (eight feet long), is capable of exerting a pressure of over 40,000 pounds per square inch, which is roughly the equivalent of having four large elephants in hobnail boots standing on your big toe.

Interesting . . .

Scientists have calculated that the speed of thought is only about 150 miles per hour.

◆　◆　◆　◆　◆

The highest recorded speed of fluid expelled by a sneeze has been measured as 103.6 mph.

According to a university study, goldfish remember better in cold water than in warm water.

◆　◆　◆　◆　◆

Goldfish will often turn white if left in a darkened room.

◆　◆　◆　◆　◆

Dolphins sleep with one eye open all the time.

◆　◆　◆　◆　◆

From the 1300's to the 1500's it was illegal for an Englishman to eat three meals a day. During the reign of Edward III in the 1300's Parliament passed a law specifying that people were to eat only two meals a day. The law remained on the books for almost 200 years.

◆　◆　◆　◆　◆

You are ¼ inch taller at night than you are during the day. The cartilage between the vertebrae of your spine gets squashed while you stand and walk around, but recovers while you sleep at night.

◆ ◆ ◆ ◆ ◆

The life expectancy of a queen termite is 50 years.

◆ ◆ ◆ ◆ ◆

Mark Twain's book "Life on the Mississippi" was the first book in history whose original manuscript was typed on a typewriter.

◆ ◆ ◆ ◆ ◆

Zane Grey is remembered as a great American writer of stories about the Wild West. However, he did much of the research for his books not out in the rugged West but in the reading room of the New York Public Library on Fifth Avenue in New York City.

◆ ◆ ◆ ◆ ◆

Most people think that sharks live only in the oceans. However, there is one very ferocious species that lives in fresh water. It is found in Lake Nicaragua in Central America.

◆ ◆ ◆ ◆ ◆

When penguins are imported to zoos in the temperate regions, they often catch colds and die. The Antarctic is so cold it's almost antiseptic, so penguins generally have not built up immunities to various germs.

◆ ◆ ◆ ◆ ◆

Birds generally take off into the wind, the same as airplanes do.

◆ ◆ ◆ ◆ ◆

Hand to Hand

There are twice as many left-handed men as left-handed women. For some unknown reason, left-handedness tends generally to be a male characteristic.

♦   ♦   ♦   ♦   ♦

After more than a year of diligent testing that consisted of (quote) "delicate food-snatching assignments," Dr. T. Michael Warren, director of the animal behavior laboratory at Penn State, has announced his conclusion that cats can be either right or left-pawed. Aside form this discovery, Dr. Warren also learned that right or left dominance is more evenly distributed in cats than in humans. Among human beings, the proportion of right-handed people to left-handed people is five to one; the proportion of right-handed to left-handed cats is more even—nine to eight.

♦   ♦   ♦   ♦   ♦

Fingernails grow faster on the right hand of right-handed people and on the left hand of left-handed people. Fingernails grow fastest on the middle finger of either hand.

♦   ♦   ♦   ♦   ♦

Some lobsters are right-handed, and some are left-handed, but almost all snails are righties, or would be if they had hands.

If you were driving down the road in Nairobi at a speed of 35 miles an hour, it is entirely possible that you might be overtaken and passed by a speeding rhinoceros.

♦   ♦   ♦   ♦   ♦

Scientists have determined that pheasants start to tremble about ten seconds before an earthquake strikes.

♦ ♦ ♦ ♦ ♦

According to a hospital study, the average new-born baby spends 113 minutes a day crying.

♦ ♦ ♦ ♦ ♦

Chewing gum while peeling onions will keep you from crying.

Going to the Dogs

The bloodhound is the only animal whose evidence is admissible in American courts.

♦ ♦ ♦ ♦ ♦

If you are going to be bitten by a dog, chances are one in four that it will be a German shepherd.

♦ ♦ ♦ ♦ ♦

Many scientists believe that the chihuahua is not really a dog. They contend that it is most likely to be a variety of rodent.

The largest single solid gold object in the world is a bathtub, of all things. It's located at the Funabara Hotel on Japan's Izu Peninsula and weighs 313½ pounds.

♦ ♦ ♦ ♦ ♦

The posh British department store, Fortnum & Mason, did an excellent business during the Crimean War providing neatly-packed picnic baskets to officers at the Battle of Sebastapol and other battle sites.

♦ ♦ ♦ ♦ ♦

The world's oldest national flag is the flag of Denmark, which has remained unchanged since about the year 1219.

♦   ♦   ♦   ♦   ♦

A Danish exporter became tired of filling out a maze of forms for every package he wanted to send to another country. To find out if anyone actually read the forms he so laboriously filled out, he began listing some highly unlikely objects in the space marked "Contents of package." Among the items he listed were "woolen stockings for elephants" and "sleeping bureaucrat." Over a period of six months, every single package got through without a customs inspector checking it.

♦   ♦   ♦   ♦   ♦

A restaurant survey has determined that people who eat the most in restaurants tend to tip the least.

♦   ♦   ♦   ♦   ♦

Tobias Smollett is remembered as one of the greatest of English satirists and writers. Among his other accomplishments was the invention of the street-corner mailbox.

♦   ♦   ♦   ♦   ♦

Abraham Lincoln has been the subject of over 8,600 books, a distinction ranking second only to Jesus.

♦   ♦   ♦   ♦   ♦

The *New York Times* was a powerful supporter of Abraham Lincoln and the effort to hold the Union together. During the Civil War there were bloody draft riots in New York City. To deter rioters from attacking the *Times*—a likely target—the editors positioned howitzers at the windows and continued to publish the newspaper. Winston Churchill's American grandfather is said to have manned one of the howitzers.

♦   ♦   ♦   ♦   ♦

Lord Laurence Olivier is acknowledged by many critics as the greatest actor of the 20th century. However, his debut as an actor was less than auspicious. His first professional role was that of a policeman in a play called *The Ghost Train*. At his first entrance—the very first time he had ever set foot on the professional stage—he tripped over the door sill and fell headfirst into the footlights. Looking back on his long and illustrious career, Olivier later claimed that he received from the audience the biggest laugh of his career.

♦   ♦   ♦   ♦   ♦

WORDS AND ODD MEANINGS

There are no turkeys in Turkey. Early explorers called the bird they found in North America a "turkey" because it reminded them of the guinea hen that comes from Asia Minor.

◆   ◆   ◆   ◆   ◆

There are over 600,000 words in the English language. A well-educated person is familiar with only about 20,000 words. In the spoken language, however, fewer than 2,000 words account for fully 99 percent of what we say. Even more astonishing is that only ten words make up 25 percent of what we say. The two most common words in the spoken language are "I" and "you."

◆　◆　◆　◆　◆

The Arabs have almost 1,000 different words for a camel.

◆　◆　◆　◆　◆

"Sequoia" is the only seven-letter word in the English language that contains all five vowels—a, e, i, o, u.

◆　◆　◆　◆　◆

The word "silly" comes from the German "selig" which means "holy." It originally referred to people who were pure and innocent, later to people who were gullible, and finally to those who are foolish and simple-minded.

◆　◆　◆　◆　◆

Most people assume that piggy banks are called "piggy banks" because they were originally made in the shape of pigs. Not so. The name comes from a ceramic material called "pygg" that was once used to make inexpensive decorative objects. An obvious object to make from pygg is, of course, a pig.

◆　◆　◆　◆　◆

When the international fast-food chain, Kentucky Fried Chicken, tried to translate its slogan, "Fingerlickin' good," into Chinese, it came out as, "Eat your fingers off." And many Asians interpreted Pepsi's "Come Alive Generation" as a call to bring back the dead.

◆　◆　◆　◆　◆

Dog Names

Boxers are called boxers because when they are excited they characteristically rise up on their hind feet and make punching motions with their front paws.

◆ ◆ ◆ ◆ ◆

Although collies are now generally tan and white, they were originally called "collies" by their Scottish breeders because the early specimens were "coalie black."

The English language is constantly changing. When the *Revised Standard Version* of the Bible was retranslated in the late 1980s, it was necessary to change some verses in the Bible that had become embarrassingly out-of-date because of changes in the American vernacular.

In the old version, the 50th psalm had a line, "I will accept no bull from your house." The *New Revised Standard* changes this line to "I will not accept a bull from your house."

In the New Testament, Paul writes to the Corinthians, "Once I was stoned . . ." but it now will read, "Once I received a stoning."

◆ ◆ ◆ ◆ ◆

Although the Bible is notably lacking in jokes and belly laughs, it does contain the phrase "Ha, ha!" (Job 39:25).

◆ ◆ ◆ ◆ ◆

In one classic American Western, the tough sheriff ambles into the saloon and tells the bar-keep, "Gimme a shot of red-eye." In France, the French subtitle translated the famous line as "Dubonnet, s'il vous plait."

◆ ◆ ◆ ◆ ◆

The words "jeans" and "denim" generally make people think of cowboys and the American Wild West. Actually denim originated in the French city of Nimes and the fabric that came from there was called "de Nimes." Genoa, Italy also produced a type of denim weave; this fabric was called "genes," which is the French word for Genoa.

◆ ◆ ◆ ◆ ◆

The French equivalent of "The quick brown fox jumped over the lazy dog" (the typing warm-up sentence containing every letter of the alphabet) is "Allez porter ce vieux whisky au juge blond qui fume un havane," meaning "Take this old whisky to the blond judge who's smoking a cigar."

◆ ◆ ◆ ◆ ◆

"Flapper," a slang term for young women during the Roaring Twenties, comes from a British word for a young duck that is too young to fly but nevertheless runs about wildly flapping its wings.

◆ ◆ ◆ ◆ ◆

The term "Ivy League" for the prestigious colleges of the Northeast such as Harvard, Princeton, and Yale is attributed to Caswell Adams, a sportswriter for the *New York Herald Tribune* in the 1930's.

When asked to compare the street-tough football team of Fordham University with those of Columbia, Princeton and other upper-class gentlemen's colleges, Adams waved his hand dismissively and sneered, "Aw, they're just ivy league schools."

Thus, the term "Ivy League," which is synonymous with prestige and accomplishment, originated as a disparaging remark.

◆ ◆ ◆ ◆ ◆

Everybody knows what the peace symbol looks like, but few people know where it comes from. The peace symbol,

an inverted Y inside a circle, was devised by British paci-
fists during the Cold War by combining the semaphore
signs for N and D, standing for nuclear disarmament.

◆　◆　◆　◆　◆

There's nothing more Scottish than the tartan. However
the word tartan itself comes from "Tartary," the name of a
region in northern China where a type of rich warm wool
fabric developed.

◆　◆　◆　◆　◆

Something's that's "tawdry" is cheap, worthless and in
poor taste. Ironically, the word comes from the name of a
saint. The saint was St. Audrey, in whose honor an annual
fair was held on the Isle of Ely. The goods sold at the fair
were of such poor quality that St. Audrey (tawdry) became synonymous with anything that was shoddily
made.

◆　◆　◆　◆　◆

The word "quiz" is said to have entered the English
language as the result of a bet. About 1780 a Dublin
theatre manager laid a wager that he could introduce a
new word into the language within 24 hours. He went
around Dublin writing the word on every blank wall. By
the next day, all of Dublin was asking what the word
meant. The theatre manager won the bet and the word
"quiz" became a permanent part of the English language.

◆　◆　◆　◆　◆

The guppy is named after Reverend R. J. Lechmere
Guppy of Trinidad, who presented the British Museum
with its first specimens of the fish in the late 19th century.

◆　◆　◆　◆　◆

Although there are similar phrases in many languages,
the expression "Your name is mud" became commonplace

in the United States shortly after the Civil War. Some scholars feel that the saying may have been inspired by the tragic story of Dr. Samuel Mudd, the doctor who set John Wilkes Booth's leg after the assassination of Abraham Lincoln. Although Mudd did not know that Booth had broken his leg during the assassination, he was nevertheless accused of being an accomplice and was sentenced to life imprisonment. He was later released, but his reputation and career were permanently ruined.

◆ ◆ ◆ ◆ ◆

The electrical terms "battery," "condenser," and "armature" were all coined by Benjamin Franklin.

◆ ◆ ◆ ◆ ◆

According to one theory, the monkey wrench (also called a spanner) was named for an inventor named Charles Moncke.

◆ ◆ ◆ ◆ ◆

The Graham cracker was invented by Sylvester Graham, a temperance leader and food fanatic who believed (among other things) that meat causes sexual excess and ketchup causes insanity.

◆ ◆ ◆ ◆ ◆

The word "poppycock," meaning "nonsense," is one of the mildest exclamations in the English language and is generally uttered by sweet little old ladies and other gentle souls. Actually, the word comes from the Dutch "papekak" meaning "soft dung."

◆ ◆ ◆ ◆ ◆

At a press conference in London, the American ambassador announced that the U.S. was "tabling" its formula for tariff cuts. To American reporters this meant that the proposed formula was being withdrawn from consideration. To British journalists, it meant exactly the opposite. In American politics, to "table" a motion is to shove it aside and forget about it; in Britain, to table a motion is to begin actively considering it.

◆　◆　◆　◆　◆

One of a horse's gaits is called a "canter." The word comes from "Canterbury," because Pilgrims supposedly used this swift gait when riding to the shrine of St. Thomas a Becket at Canterbury.

◆　◆　◆　◆　◆

The catch phrase "right-on," appears in Shakespeare's "Julius Caesar" (Act 3, Scene 2).

◆　◆　◆　◆　◆

◆ 4 ◆
AT THE MOVIES

Actress Bette Davis claimed that it was she who gave the Academy Award statuette the nickname "Oscar." She said that the nude statuette's backside reminded her of that of her first husband. Her first husband was Harmon Oscar Nelson, who, incidentally, was often called "Ham" by those who knew him. Fortunately, the statue that actors covet so deeply was called "Oscar" rather than "Ham."

◆　◆　◆　◆　◆

To conserve metal, the "Oscars" given out in the Academy Award ceremony during World War II were made of wood.

♦   ♦   ♦   ♦   ♦

In 1926, Rin Tin Tin was voted "Most Popular Film Performer of the Year," beating out the likes of Charlie Chaplin, Clara Bow, Rudolph Valentino, Theda Bara and Douglas Fairbanks.

Funny Men

Comedian Danny Kaye made his schoolboy stage debut as a watermelon seed.

♦   ♦   ♦   ♦

In their movies together, Laurel and Hardy always played two likeable buffoons. Before the two of them got together however, Oliver Hardy generally played villainous "bad guys."

♦   ♦   ♦   ♦   ♦

Comedian Lou Costello, the roly-poly member of the comedy team of Abbott and Costello, once worked as a prizefighter. In his early days at MGM, he was a stunt man and once worked as Dolores del Rio's double.

♦   ♦   ♦   ♦   ♦

W.C. Fields once worked as a professional "drowner" for the owner of a concession stand in Atlantic City, New Jersey. Fields would swim out into the ocean and pretend he was drowning. A crowd would gather while he was being rescued and revived. The concession owner would sell hot dogs and ice cream to the throng and split the profits with Fields.

In the *Star Wars* movies, the character Luke Skywalker originally had the name "Luke Skykiller," but the producer decided the name didn't sound wholesome enough.

◆ ◆ ◆ ◆ ◆

The classic movie thriller *Psycho* was inspired by a macabre real-life event that occurred in a small town in Minnesota in 1957.

Ed Gein was a soft-spoken, hard-working handyman who never cursed, smoked, or drank. His entire life was dominated by his stern, repressive mother, Augusta, and after her death he turned her room into a shrine.

In the fall of 1957, a policeman, investigating the disappearance of a local shopkeeper, checked up on the last purchase listed in her receipt book—the sale of a can of antifreeze to Ed Gein.

The policeman went to Gein's farmhouse to talk to him about it, and discovered the woman's body, stripped and decapitated, hung by the heels from a rafter. Further investigation revealed ten female "masks," fashioned from actual faces gleaned from ghoulish nighttime visits to the cemetery. The policeman recognized one of the masks as the face of another woman who had disappeared three years before.

In 1974, Gein claimed that he had recovered his sanity and made an unsuccessful attempt to be released from a mental hospital.

He died in 1984 and was buried in an unmarked grave next to his beloved mother.

◆ ◆ ◆ ◆ ◆

Buster Keaton, whose first crib was his parents' vaudeville trunk, made his debut at the tender age of four, stoically enduring his parents' brutal comedy routines, which often verged on outright child abuse.

He got the nickname, Buster, from fellow vaudevillian Harry Houdini, who marvelled at the young child's toughness and stoicism in the face of abuse.

In the 1920s Keaton was one of Hollywood's biggest stars until his career was ruined by his alcoholism. By the early 1930's, he was scraping by as an uncredited gag writer for the Marx Brothers and Red Skelton and soon sank into obscurity.

His comic genius was "rediscovered" after a 1957 article in *Life Magazine*, and he found new fame and appreciation in films, television and even in an experimental piece written by Samuel Beckett.

When he died in 1966, he was buried with a rosary in one pocket and a deck of cards in the other, so he would be prepared, whichever direction he was headed.

◆ ◆ ◆ ◆ ◆

Actor Sean Connery once worked as a coffin-polisher.

◆ ◆ ◆ ◆ ◆

Albert ("Cubby") Broccoli, the phenomenally-successful producer of the James Bond movies, was once a coffin salesman. He's also related to the man who introduced broccoli to America.

◆ ◆ ◆ ◆ ◆

Author Ian Fleming's top four choices for an actor to portray James Bond on the screen included the gangly American actor James Stewart as well as Richard Burton, David Niven, and James Mason.

◆ ◆ ◆ ◆ ◆

Composer John Barry was paid less than $500 for coming up with the distinctive plucked guitar theme of the Bond movies.

◆ ◆ ◆ ◆ ◆

Actor Humphrey Bogart was famous for his expressionless face and rasping lisp. Both of these characteristics were the result of a war wound. While he was serving in the military during World War I, his troopship was shelled by the Germans. Although he recovered from his wounds, he was left with a permanent partial paralysis of his upper lip.

◆ ◆ ◆ ◆ ◆

The actress Tuesday Weld was born on a Friday.

◆ ◆ ◆ ◆ ◆

Charles Boyer's most famous line was "Come with me to the Casbah." Jimmy Cagney was famous for "You dirty rat"; Greta Garbo for "I vant to be alone"; and Humphrey Bogart for "Play it again, Sam."
The ironic thing is that none of these actors ever spoke the lines that are now so closely identified with them.

◆ ◆ ◆ ◆ ◆

At one time, Sophia Loren was related by marriage to the dictator, Benito Mussolini. Her sister was once married to Mussolini's son.

◆ ◆ ◆ ◆ ◆

In 1927, the silent movie actress Norma Talmadge started a Hollywood tradition when she blundered into a patch of wet cement outside of Grauman's Chinese Theatre in Hollywood. Since then, hundreds of movie stars have had their footprints and handprints enshrined in the cement outside the theatre. What began as a clumsy accident has resulted in the elevation of the theatre of one of Los Angeles' foremost tourist attractions.

◆ ◆ ◆ ◆ ◆

In the filming of *Gone with the Wind*, the baby who portrayed Scarlett O'Hara's baby daughter, Bonnie Blue Butler, was actually a male infant named Greg Geiss. Mr.

Geiss was paid $95 for his role. Another man, a 35-year old stunt double, dressed up as Bonnie Blue for the scene in which she is killed in a fall from her pony.

Movie Bloopers

In the John Wayne movie, *The Green Berets*, there's a scene that supposedly takes place on the eastern coast of Vietnam, showing the sun setting over the Pacific. The only problem with the scene is that, in Vietnam and everywhere else, the sun sets in the west.

The fact that movie makers are occasionally ignorant of basic geography can also be seen in the title of the movie, *Krakatoa, East of Java*. The famous volcanic island of Krakatoa is, and always has been, west of Java.

◆　◆　◆　◆　◆

After spending tremendous sums of money to hire thousands of extras for a huge crowd scene in *El Cid*, a movie extravaganza set in the 11th century, the film editors were horrified to discover that one extra in the scene was wearing sunglasses.

◆　◆　◆　◆　◆

Another famous movie mistake occurs in a scene in *The King and I*. Yul Brynner is seen wearing an earring in some camera shots and no earring in other camera shots.

◆　◆　◆　◆　◆

In the classic film, *The Invisible Man*, there is another blooper. The footprints of the man (who is invisible because he is naked) are the prints of shoes rather than bare feet.

Actor John Wayne once won Lassie in a poker game, but later felt bad and gave the dog back to her owner.

♦   ♦   ♦   ♦   ♦

When actress Katharine Hepburn married a man named Ludlow Ogden Smith in 1928, she made him change his last name so that she wouldn't have the same last name as the singer Kate Smith.

♦   ♦   ♦   ♦   ♦

Actor Stewart Granger's real name was Jimmy Stewart. Actor Jimmy Stewart's real name is Jimmy Stewart.

♦   ♦   ♦   ♦   ♦

In the famous 1944 movie *To Have and Have Not* actress Lauren Bacall's singing voice was dubbed in by a 14-year-old boy who grew up to become the famous singing star, Andy Williams.

♦   ♦   ♦   ♦   ♦

The Tarzan yell made famous in the Johnny Weissmuller films was created in a sound studio from a number of different sounds. The sound technicians blended a camel's bleat and a hyena's yowl and played it backwards. To that was added the sound of a plucked violin, a soprano's high C, and Weissmuller howling at the top of his lungs, with each sound played a fraction of a second after the other. It took a lot of practice for Weissmuller to learn how to do an acceptable imitation of the synthetically-produced sound effect during personal appearance tours.

♦   ♦   ♦   ♦   ♦

◆ 5 ◆
MALE AND FEMALE

From infancy on, men tend to laugh more than women.

◆　◆　◆　◆　◆

According to an extensive study, a man is twice as likely to fall out of a hospital bed as a woman.

◆　◆　◆　◆　◆

Women throw balls differently from men because their arms are constructed differently. A women's arm tends to be longer from the elbow to the shoulder than it is from the wrist to the elbow. The length of a man's forearm is usually greater than the length of his upper arm.

◆ ◆ ◆ ◆ ◆

The I.Q. range among men is greater than that among women. The most stupid men tend to be stupider than the stupidest women and the smartest men smarter than the smartest women. A greater percentage of men have genius-level I.Q.s than women. However, males are also more likely to be born mentally retarded.

◆ ◆ ◆ ◆ ◆

If a man and a woman of equal size and weight go to a cocktail party and drink exactly the same amount of liquor, the woman is far more likely to become intoxicated. Men have a greater percentage of water in their body tissues than women do. The extra water dilutes the alcohol in the bloodstream faster.

◆ ◆ ◆ ◆ ◆

The heart of an unborn baby girl beats faster than the heart of an unborn baby boy.

◆ ◆ ◆ ◆ ◆

Women breathe faster than men.

◆ ◆ ◆ ◆ ◆

If you took a man and a woman of the same height and similar body type, the man would invariably weigh more. A man has almost twice as much muscle tissue as even the most physically fit woman. A woman has more fatty tissue, which weighs much less than muscle tissue.

◆ ◆ ◆ ◆ ◆

Since women have more fatty tissue in their bodies, they have a distinct advantage over men in certain swimming events. They are more buoyant in the water and it takes less effort for them to swim. Since fatty tissue helps insulate the body against cold, women are better able to swim long distances in cold water than men are.

♦ ♦ ♦ ♦ ♦

On a man's shirt the buttonholes are on the left side of his garment and the buttons on his right. It's exactly the opposite on a woman's blouse.

Most people are right-handed. Throughout history men of all social classes have generally dressed themselves. The button arrangement on men's clothes makes it easy for most men (most are right-handed) to dress themselves. However, hundreds of years ago women of the noble classes were dressed by their maids, so the buttons were arranged to make it easy for a right-handed servant to dress her employer. The button arrangement filtered down to the lower classes and became standard on all women's clothes.

♦ ♦ ♦ ♦ ♦

People often claim that men in industrialized countries have a lower life expectancy than women because of the stress of modern business life. Not true. In every country in the world, industrialized or not, the average life span of a woman is significantly greater than that of a man.

♦ ♦ ♦ ♦ ♦

A study by the American Bar Association found that young girls who are accused of minor crimes tend to receive harsher sentences than boys who are convicted of more serious crimes.

♦ ♦ ♦ ♦ ♦

At least one man a year has drowned in the popular Long Island, New York, lake, Lake Ronkonkoma. However, there is no record of a *woman* ever drowing there.

♦   ♦   ♦   ♦   ♦

According to a psychological study, women talk about men three times as much as men talk about women.

♦   ♦   ♦   ♦   ♦

You can find out whether a mosquito is male or female by letting it land on you. If it bites you, it's female. Only female mosquitos live on blood. The males live on plant juices.

♦   ♦   ♦   ♦   ♦

A researcher at the Museum of Natural History in New York has announced that she has discovered that male cockroaches stay out later at night than female cockroaches.

♦   ♦   ♦   ♦   ♦

They say that diamonds are a girl's best friend. However, diamonds were generally worn only by men until the 15th century.

♦   ♦   ♦   ♦   ♦

When the Washington Monument opened in 1888, men took the elevator but women were required to climb the 897 steps of the memorial. It was thought improper for men to accompany women in such an enclosed space for the 12 minutes that the elevator took to rise to the top of the 555-foot-tall monument.

♦   ♦   ♦   ♦   ♦

◆ 6 ◆

MISTAKES, MISNOMERS AND OTHER MISINFORMATION

The idea that Cinderella wore glass slippers is the result of a mistranslation. In the early French versions of the story, Cinderella's shoes were made of fur. The French words for "squirrel fur" (vair) and "glass" (verre) are so similar that when the tale was translated into English the translator mistakenly called it a glass slipper. The mistake has probably made the story far more charming. A glass slipper is somewhat more romantic than a furry moccasin.

♦ ♦ ♦ ♦ ♦

Black-eyed peas aren't peas. They're beans. On the other hand, coffee beans aren't beans. They are actually fruit pits.

♦ ♦ ♦ ♦ ♦

The so-called "Panama hat" actually originated in Ecuador.

♦ ♦ ♦ ♦ ♦

So-called India ink does not come from India. It's from China.

Calendar Confusion

Russia's "October Revolution" took place in November according to the Gregorian calendar, which Russia did not adopt until 1918.

♦ ♦ ♦ ♦ ♦

Germany's two-week long celebration called the "Oktoberfest" takes place almost entirely in September.

♦ ♦ ♦ ♦ ♦

September was the seventh month of the Roman calendar, October was the eighth, November the ninth and December the tenth. When Julius Caesar named July after himself and Augustus named August for himself (see page 95) and inserted these as the seventh and eighth months of our calendar year, the later months were moved up two months.

In 1849, a British mapmaker on an expedition to Alaska was working on a chart of the Alaskan coast. He noticed that none of the maps he had available listed the name of a prominent cape along the coastline. He made a notation "Name?" on the map, intending that the mapmaking company back in London should check on the correct name of the cape. However, a draftsman at the mapmaking company misread the notation, thinking that it meant the name of the cape was "Nome." The city has been known as Nome, Alaska, ever since.

♦   ♦   ♦   ♦   ♦

When Portuguese explorers sailed into a big beautiful bay on the east coast of South America in January of 1503, they mistakenly assumed that the bay was the mouth of a great river. It isn't. Nevertheless, the place still bears the erroneous name Rio de Janeiro, which means "River of January."

♦   ♦   ♦   ♦   ♦

Author Thomas Carlyle gave the only copy of the manuscript of his great book *The French Revolution* to John Stuart Mill for Mill to read and evaluate. While Mill was away, his housekeeper made the horrifying mistake of using the manuscript to light a fire. The only copy of the entire first volume was destroyed and Carlyle had to start over again.

♦   ♦   ♦   ♦   ♦

Lawrence of Arabia is another literary "loser." He lost the manuscript for his book *The Seven Pillars of Wisdom* and had to rewrite the entire thing from memory.

♦   ♦   ♦   ♦   ♦

The poet Carl Sandburg received an appointment in 1899 to West Point but he was kicked out before becoming a plebe. The reason? He failed written tests in grammar, as well as arithmetic. Despite the military's low opinion of his writing skills, he went on to become one of the world's great poets.

Eating Your Words

Spanish rice was not invented in Spain.

♦   ♦   ♦   ♦   ♦

English muffins were not invented in England.

♦   ♦   ♦   ♦   ♦

Danish pastries were not invented in Denmark.

♦   ♦   ♦   ♦   ♦

Russian dressing is unknown in Russia.

♦   ♦   ♦   ♦   ♦

Welsh rabbit is not made with rabbit; it's melted cheese on bread.

♦   ♦   ♦   ♦   ♦

Bombay duck is not a duck; it's made with dry fish and curry.

♦   ♦   ♦   ♦   ♦

Cape Cod turkey isn't turkey; it's a slang term for a codfish.

The tea bag was invented by mistake in 1904 when a tea merchant passed out samples of tea wrapped in little silk bags. People didn't understand that the merchant meant for them to open the bags. They found it convenient and tidy just to dunk the whole bag into the water and soon came back to the surprised "inventor" clamoring for more of his "tea bags."

◆   ◆   ◆   ◆   ◆

"Wheaties" were invented by accident. In 1921, a dietitian mixing a batch of bran gruel for his patients spilled some on a hot stove top. He brought the resulting flakes to the cereal company who immediately agreed that the concoction had all the nutritional value of bran gruel but a much better taste. Which would you rather have for breakfast, "Wheaties" or bran gruel?

◆   ◆   ◆   ◆   ◆

The famous ocean liner "Queen Mary" is said to have been named as the result of a misunderstanding. The Cunard Line had planned to name the ship "Queen Victoria."

A representative from the company visited King George V and began to explain to him that Cunard wanted to name its new ship after one of Great Britain's greatest queens. The king interrupted, saying how pleased Queen Mary would be. The company had no choice but to name the ship the "Queen Mary."

◆   ◆   ◆   ◆   ◆

Turkish towels aren't Turkish. They're French.

◆   ◆   ◆   ◆   ◆

Tennessee Williams was born in Mississippi.

◆   ◆   ◆   ◆   ◆

Although matinees are invariably held in the afternoon, the word "matinee" comes from the French for "morning."

◆   ◆   ◆   ◆   ◆

The American Beauty Rose is French, not American. It was first bred in France and named the Madame Ferdinand Jamin. Later, entrepreneurs renamed it the American Beauty to increase sales in the United States.

♦ ♦ ♦ ♦ ♦

Spanish moss is neither moss nor Spanish.

♦ ♦ ♦ ♦ ♦

The funny bone is not a bone. It is a nerve.

♦ ♦ ♦ ♦ ♦

The English walnut is not English. It is Persian.

The Truth About The Old West

In cowboy films, the hero often appears to get 10 or 12 shots off from his "six-shooter" before he has to reload. Actually, it would be a mistake to show a cowboy getting off six shots, because real cowboys almost never kept six bullets in their guns. Early revolvers did not have a safety catch so a smart cowboy generally left one chamber empty so that he wouldn't go through the pain and embarrassment of shooting himself in the foot.

♦ ♦ ♦ ♦ ♦

The so-called 10-gallon hat holds only about 3 quarts.

Believe it or not, "Ripley's Believe It or Not" was not written by Robert Ripley—he was an artist. The column was written almost entirely by Norbert Pearlroth and Douglas Storer for over 50 years. Although Ripley has been dead since 1950, the column still bears his name— even though he never wrote it in the first place.

♦ ♦ ♦ ♦ ♦

"Don't Call Us ..."

In the early 1930's, a Hollywood producer turned down a cute little girl named Shirley Temple for a long-term contract in the *Our Gang* series of comedy films.

◆ ◆ ◆ ◆ ◆

It is said that there is not a moment of the day when reruns of the madcap television series *I Love Lucy* are not playing somewhere in the world. Lucille Ball's career didn't start off so well, however. She was once dismissed from drama school for being too quiet and shy.

◆ ◆ ◆ ◆ ◆

Some of the greatest dance sequences in the history of the movies have been created and performed by actor-dancer Fred Astaire, who earned an Academy Award "for his unique artistry and his contribution to the techniques of motion pictures." This contrasts ironically with the report on his first screen test for MGM that read: "Can't act, slightly bald, can dance a little."

◆ ◆ ◆ ◆ ◆

When he was in the eighth grade, Elvis Presley had a music teacher in school who wrote a report stating that he showed little promise as a musician. After his first appearance at the Grand Ole Opry in Nashville, the talent manager of the theatre told him that he should consider going into the career of driving a truck. It's been estimated that he grossed over $100,000,000 during his first two years of stardom and never earned less than $4,000,000 a year during the rest of his life.

The American coin called the "nickel" is actually mostly copper. The metal the coin is made from is 75 percent copper and only 25 percent nickel.

♦ ♦ ♦ ♦ ♦

The so-called "English horn" is neither English nor a horn. The word "horn" is generally restricted to brass instruments; the English horn is a woodwind. Also, it developed on the continent, not in England.

♦ ♦ ♦ ♦ ♦

John Sutter, the owner of Sutter's Mill, where the California gold rush of 1849 started, made the mistake of letting news of the discovery leak out. His land was quickly taken over by squatters and his sheep and cattle were stolen. Although many others made fortunes during the gold rush, Sutter, the man who started it all, went bankrupt three years later and lived out his last years on a modest government pension.

♦ ♦ ♦ ♦ ♦

There is no lead in so-called "lead pencils" and never has been. A lead pencil is mostly made with graphite.

♦ ♦ ♦ ♦ ♦

The motto on American coins is "In God We Trust." However, the U.S. mint once made a terrible mistake on a run of gold coins: each coin had the phrase "In Gold We Trust" stamped on it.

♦ ♦ ♦ ♦ ♦

◆7◆

BIZARRE ...

Ex-Beatle Paul McCartney paid over 110 pounds (nearly $200) to have a taxicab drive his pet chickens from London to his home in Scotland. His wife and children were vactioning with him in Scotland when Mr. McCartney realized that there was no one at home in London to feed his beloved chickens. Mr. McCartney immediately hired a taxi from London. The chickens made the journey in comfort, fluttering around in the back seat of a taxi.

◆ ◆ ◆ ◆ ◆

The Brookings Institution is a world-famous "think tank" in Washington, D.C. It does research into the most complicated and complex problems that face mankind. Ironically, its founder, multi-millionaire Robert S. Brookings, made his fortune in a somewhat less complicated field, the manufacturing of clothespins.

◆ ◆ ◆ ◆ ◆

In A.D. 60, the Olympics hit a new low in standards of skill, sportsmanship and integrity when the Roman emperor Nero entered as a contestant. Nero was a terrible athlete, but he was also one of the most politically powerful men in the ancient world and great efforts were made not to injure his ego. He was judged the winner in every event he entered.

◆ ◆ ◆ ◆ ◆

When the wife of the English poet and artist, Dante Rossetti, died in 1862, he was so overwhelmed by emotion that, in a flamboyant burst of poetic sentiment, he buried the only copy of an unpublished manuscript of love sonnets in her coffin. Later on, he thought better of the whole thing and had his wife dug up. The sonnets were published in 1870, netting the poet a tidy little profit.

◆ ◆ ◆ ◆ ◆

A ship weighs less when the moon is directly overhead.

◆ ◆ ◆ ◆ ◆

One of the most remarkable coincidences in history is an 1898 novel by Morgan Robertson that "foretold" the sinking of the *Titanic* 14 years before the disaster occurred. There is astonishing similarity between Robertson's fictional ship and the real *Titanic*. In the novel, Robertson describes his ship as having a displacement of 70,000 tons; the *Titanic's* displacement was only 4,000 tons less. The two ships had similar passenger capacities (about 3,000), top speed (25 knots), length (800 feet vs. 882.5 feet) and they shared numerous other features, including the lack of a sufficient number of lifeboats.

In the novel, Robertson's ship, which has a passenger list filled with wealthy and powerful people, is on its maiden voyage when it strikes an iceberg in the North Atlantic on an April night and sinks.

The *Titanic*, which was also on its maiden voyage, struck an iceberg in the North Atlantic on the night of April 12, 1912 and sank, carrying some of the most prominent people in the world to their deaths.

The name of Robertson's fictional ship? . . . The *Titan*.

◆   ◆   ◆   ◆   ◆

The 11th-century religious leader St. Bernard once excommunicated a swarm of flies for buzzing too loudly while he was preaching.

◆   ◆   ◆   ◆   ◆

According to an extensive study carried out in California in 1966, pigs are the only mammals other than man that are capable of getting sunburned.

◆   ◆   ◆   ◆   ◆

A government-financed research project determined that pigs can become alcoholics.

◆   ◆   ◆   ◆   ◆

In medieval days, even dogs wore suits of armor.

◆   ◆   ◆   ◆   ◆

The Greek practice of ostracism or banishment was introduced and promoted by the Athenian statesman

Clisthenes. According to legend, the first person to be ostracized from Athens was Clisthenes himself.

◆ ◆ ◆ ◆ ◆

In 1923, the U.S. Supreme Court overturned a Nebraska law, passed in a surge of nativist emotion after World War I, that made it a *crime* to teach foreign languages to young children.

◆ ◆ ◆ ◆ ◆

The great American poet, Hart Crane, who deliberately drowned himself by jumping overboard from a ship in 1933, was the son of the inventor of "Lifesavers" candy.

◆ ◆ ◆ ◆ ◆

Up until 1987, unmarried couples who lived together in Massachusetts could be punished by being taken to the gallows and made to stand there with a rope around their necks, receiving 39 lashes. The town of Sharon, Massachusetts, threatened to cite the 1784 law against two of its employees, and it took an act of the State Legislature to get the law off the books.

◆ ◆ ◆ ◆ ◆

The first autopsy in the New World was performed in Santo Domingo in 1533 upon a pair of Siamese twins. The purpose of the autopsy had nothing to do with science or medicine, but rather, religion, because the priest wanted to know if he was dealing with one soul or two. Based on the autopsy, he decided there were two separate souls.

Chang and Eng, born in Siam in 1811, became famous throughout the world, forever identifying their condition as "Siamese twins"—despite the fact that they were born of Chinese, not Siamese, parents.

Chang and Eng had strikingly disparate personalities: good-natured Eng played chess and was a teetotaler; Chang liked to paint the town red, often drank himself into alcoholic stupors and had to be bribed to sit still while Eng played chess. In 1843 they married two sisters who lived down the road from their North Carolina farm. The sisters feuded bitterly, so the quartet set up two different households: the twins spent half their nights sleeping with one sister and the other half sleeping with the other. This unlikely marriage resulted in a total of 22 children.

♦ ♦ ♦ ♦ ♦

One of the most bizarre sieges in history was the assault upon the Egyptian city of Memphis by King Cambyses II of Persia. The city walls were thick and high and the Persians were unable to penetrate the city's defenses. Then Cambyses got a brilliant idea.

The Egyptians treated cats as if they were divine creatures and gave them all sorts of homage. The Persians, however, thought that cats were simply cats and not worthy of any special attention.

The Persians rounded up every cat they could find and began lobbing them over the walls to their deaths. The Egyptians were horrified to see their divine creatures being used as living cannonballs. Rather than let more cats die, they promptly surrendered.

♦ ♦ ♦ ♦ ♦

Ravel's great musical piece, "Bolero," was inspired by a trip to a noisy steel mill.

♦ ♦ ♦ ♦ ♦

In a study of attitudes towards body weight among 26 of the world's cultures, only five reported a preference for thin men. America, of course, led the list. In the English-speaking cultures, there is a distinct correlation between attitudes towards body weight and the social class you belong to. A burly, potbellied body tends to command respect among blue-collar workers, but attitudes tend to change in direct proportion to wealth and status. Compare this to other places such as Samoa, where a man must weigh at least 400 pounds to qualify as tribal king.

◆   ◆   ◆   ◆   ◆

Catherine de Medici, Queen of France during the 16th century, was one of the great masters in the art of poisoning. She was also one of the first practitioners of the modern technique of systematic product testing. She tested her latest poisons by delivering neatly wrapped food baskets to the poor. By carefully noting the effects of various combinations of poisonous substances, she was able to hone her art to ever greater heights of deadliness.

◆   ◆   ◆   ◆   ◆

In the 14th century, the wife of Dom Pedro, the heir to the throne of Portugal, was stabbed to death in a court intrigue. When Dom Pedro finally gained the throne several years later, he had his wife's body dug up and placed on the throne beside him. All the noblemen of the court were ordered to bow and kiss the hand of the dead queen.

◆   ◆   ◆   ◆   ◆

— ◆ 8 ◆ —
ODD JOBS

Wild West hero Kit Carson worked as a saddler's apprentice as a youth. Apparently, he was not a very good worker. When he ran away from his job to seek his fortune out west, his employer offered a 1¢ reward for his return.

◆ ◆ ◆ ◆ ◆

Peter Mark Roget, the author of the famous *Roget's Thesaurus*, was a doctor by profession. Working in his spare time, it took him *fifty* years to finish the book.

◆ ◆ ◆ ◆ ◆

The labor union movement reached its high point decades ago in the U.S. However, it wasn't until a strike in 1977 that the Hamill Manufacturing Company of Imlay City, Michigan, agreed to stop requiring its assembly line employees to raise their hands for permission to go to the bathroom.

◆ ◆ ◆ ◆ ◆

The first recorded labor strike took place in 1160 B.C. when laborers on Pharaoh Rameses III tomb went on strike to demand a cost of living increase.

◆ ◆ ◆ ◆ ◆

The world's longest strike occurred at Dun Laoghaire, Ireland, in protest over the firing of a bartender. The Barman's Union called the strike on March 6, 1939 and daily picketing continued for almost 15 years until the strike was settled with a new owner on December 5, 1954.

Served Them Right

The Communist leader Karl Marx worked as a columnist for the *New York Tribune* in the mid-1800's. He contributed analyses of European politics for eleven years until he got into a dispute with Horace Greeley, the famous editor of the *Tribune*. Greeley apparently misunderstood Marx' comments on the evil of money in capitalist societies and thought he could get away with cutting Marx' salary from $10 to $5 a week. Marx promptly quit and refused ever to write another word for the *Tribune*.

As Machiavelli said, "It is not titles that honor men; but men that honor titles." In Moline, Illinois, garbage men are now referred to as "garbologists"; in some areas of England, they are called "swill solicitors." The title sometimes preferred by janitors is "sanitorians." Many lowly messengers have had the loftly title "communications couriers." And finally, barroom bouncers now bear the more genteel title "crowd control engineers."

◆   ◆   ◆   ◆   ◆

Thomas Edison's first invention was a device that enabled him to sleep on the job. As a young man, he worked as a telegraph operator. He was required periodically to check the wires by sending a brief signal to another station once every hour throughout the night. He devised a gadget that sent the signal automatically so that he could sleep undisturbed.

◆   ◆   ◆   ◆   ◆

The French painter Gauguin worked on the Panama Canal in 1887.

◆   ◆   ◆   ◆   ◆

Thomas Paine, the English-born pamphleteer of both the American and French Revolutions, once worked as a ladies' girdle-maker.

◆   ◆   ◆   ◆   ◆

Garibaldi, the great Italian leader, once worked as a candle-maker on Staten Island in New York.

◆   ◆   ◆   ◆   ◆

The first collaboration of the great musical team of Lerner and Loewe (*My Fair Lady*), was a 1942 farce called *Life of the Party*. It ran a total of one performance.

Although Frederick Loewe was from a prominent Viennese musical family, when he came to the United States to achieve musical fame, he wound up out west prospecting for gold and working as a cowboy.

♦ ♦ ♦ ♦ ♦

American Wild West hero Bat Masterson spent his later years as a newspaper reporter in New York City. The tough gunfighter is buried in the "Primrose" section of Woodlawn Cemetery in the Bronx.

♦ ♦ ♦ ♦ ♦

Studies show that university professors who smoke are twice as likely to write textbooks.

♦ ♦ ♦ ♦ ♦

The philosopher Henry David Thoreau once worked as Ralph Waldo Emerson's gardener.

♦ ♦ ♦ ♦ ♦

According to studies by Dr. August Dvorak of the University of Washington, a typist's fingers travel a total of seven miles during a seven-hour workday.

♦ ♦ ♦ ♦ ♦

The mentally-imbalanced author Edgar Allan Poe and LSD advocate Timothy Leary both attended the U.S. Military Academy at West Point.

♦ ♦ ♦ ♦ ♦

◆ 9 ◆

THAT'S SURPRISING ...

If the time period from the beginning of the universe to the present time were compressed into the span of a single year, dinosaurs would still be roaming the earth on Christmas Day and all the history in the world from the Renaissance to the present day would take place in the last *second* of New Year's Eve.

◆　◆　◆　◆　◆

From 1659 to 1681, it was illegal to celebrate Christmas in Massachusetts.

Anatomy Lesson

Your head weighs about 12 pounds. An adult skull is made of solid bone. A child, however, has a skull that is made up of 29 separate bones.

♦ ♦ ♦ ♦ ♦

There is no exact figure on the number of bones in the human body. Scientists have found many variations in individual people. Some people have an extra vertebra; some an extra rib. Adults generally have about 206 bones. Children, however, have 350, which are fused together during their early years.

♦ ♦ ♦ ♦ ♦

A 150-pound person contains about 145 pounds of water, protein, and stored fat; the rest is minerals, acids and chemicals.

♦ ♦ ♦ ♦ ♦

The basic chemicals in the human body are worth only a few dollars. However, a Yale biochemist, Harold J. Morowitz, says that you're actually worth much more than that. He estimates that it would cost six million dollars to manufacture the intricate hormones, proteins and enzymes in your body. The task of fashioning these raw materials into human cells might cost six thousand trillion dollars. The cost of putting the cells together to create a human being is beyond comprehension.

According to a scientific paper on the nutritional value of cannibalism, a 150-pound man would yield about 90 pounds of edible muscle mass if skilfully butchered. This is enough to cater a sit-down dinner for 75 people.

◆　◆　◆　◆　◆

During your lifetime, you eat about 60,000 pounds of food, the equivalent in weight of six elephants.

Bearded

A scientific survey has discovered that American men's beard growth is greatest on Wednesdays and smallest on Sundays. There is no explanation for this phenomenon.

◆　◆　◆　◆　◆

During the reign of Queen Elizabeth I, a law was passed that made men with beards pay a special tax.

◆　◆　◆　◆　◆

Contrary to what you would expect, blond beards grow faster than dark beards.

During a blizzard in Buffalo, New York, a course in arctic survival techniques was cancelled due to inclement weather.

◆　◆　◆　◆　◆

The temperature of your hands and feet can drop to 40 degrees below normal without lasting harm.

◆　◆　◆　◆　◆

Of the five senses, the sense that diminishes most rapidly as you get older is your sense of smell.

◆　◆　◆　◆　◆

According to a university study, young people have a greater tolerance for pain than older people.

◆　◆　◆　◆　◆

A great milestone of Western civilization was reached in 1920 when, through the wonders of medical science, the average life expectancy of man finally surpassed that of the goldfish. Prior to 1920, the life expectancy of a man was 48.4 years, as compared to over 50 years for certain breeds of wild goldfish, which belong to the carp family.

◆　◆　◆　◆　◆

The life span of a caveman averaged only about 18 years. The ancient Romans lived to be about 22 years old. The Egyptians did a little better, with an average life span of 29 years. Several thousand years later in 1850, the average life span in the civilized world was still only about 37 years. Today the average life span is over 70 years in most industrialized nations.

◆　◆　◆　◆　◆

Many anthropologists think that prehistoric man sang long before he developed the ability to communicate by speech.

◆　◆　◆　◆　◆

Julia Ward Howe sold her rights to the lyrics to the American patriotic song "The Battle Hymn of the Republic" to a magazine for four dollars.

◆　◆　◆　◆　◆

Rimsky-Korsakov's famous musical piece "Capriccio Espagnol" has a title that is half-Italian and half-French. Oddly enough, it was written about Spain by a Russian.

◆　◆　◆　◆　◆

In a strange trial in 1923, the Westman Publishing Company, which published the sheet music from Handel's "Messiah," sued the writers of the nonsense song "Yes, We Have No Bananas," claiming the melody was stolen directly from their copyrighted arrangement of Handel's "Messiah." They won.

◆ ◆ ◆ ◆ ◆

Unborn babies dream.

Out of the Pantry

When building a bridge, one of the ingredients you need is sugar. Sugar is added to the mortar because tests show that it increases the mortar's strength.

◆ ◆ ◆ ◆ ◆

Aside from being a popular food product, peanuts are also used in the production of dynamite.

◆ ◆ ◆ ◆ ◆

Instant coffee is thought of as a very modern thing. However, it has been around since 1838.

◆ ◆ ◆ ◆ ◆

Coffee was considered an aphrodisiac in the 18th century.

In the famous race between the early locomotive "Tom Thumb" and a horse, the *horse* won. The purpose of the race was to demonstrate the speed and reliability of this new mode of transportation. Unfortunately, the historic race ended when a belt slipped and the Tom Thumb came to a dead stop, thus ushering in a new age of grumbling passengers.

◆ ◆ ◆ ◆ ◆

The Liberty Bell and Big Ben were both cast by the same English foundry.

♦   ♦   ♦   ♦   ♦

The flag of Italy was designed by Napoleon Bonaparte.

♦   ♦   ♦   ♦   ♦

Michelangelo designed the uniforms of the famous Swiss Guards at the Vatican during the 1500's. The uniforms remained unchanged for 450 years until 1975 when, in keeping with the times, the guards were issued a new piece of equipment: tear gas grenades.

♦   ♦   ♦   ♦   ♦

The famous French artist Maurice Utrillo began painting at the age of 17 as therapy for his adolescent alcoholism.

♦   ♦   ♦   ♦   ♦

Only about 80,000 tons of gold have been mined since the dawn of civilization—a mass equal in weight to the amount of metal the American steel industry can produce in two hours.

♦   ♦   ♦   ♦   ♦

Thomas Edison's schooling was limited to three months in Port Huron, Michigan, in 1854.

♦   ♦   ♦   ♦   ♦

The works of mystery writer Agatha Christie have been translated into more languages than the plays of Shakespeare.

♦   ♦   ♦   ♦   ♦

When you sail from the Atlantic to the Pacific through the Panama Canal, you are travelling in an *easterly* direction. The canal is located at a curve in the isthmus of Panama and the Atlantic entrance is farther west than the Pacific entrance.

◆   ◆   ◆   ◆   ◆

The phrase "as solid as the Rock of Gibraltar" is not quite accurate. Actually, the Rock is riddled with hundreds of natural limestone caverns and artificial tunnels and caves.

◆   ◆   ◆   ◆   ◆

At their closest point, the United States and Russia are less than two miles apart.

◆   ◆   ◆   ◆   ◆

More than 40 percent of the Netherlands was once covered by the sea or by lakes or swamps. It's appropriate, therefore, that a standard unit of area in Holland is called a "mud." It's equal to about 2½ acres.

◆   ◆   ◆   ◆   ◆

Only about three percent of the water on the Earth is fresh, and of that, 75 percent is frozen in polar icecaps and glaciers.

◆   ◆   ◆   ◆   ◆

Lake Baikal in southern Siberia is estimated to contain as much as one fifth of the world's supply of fresh water.

◆   ◆   ◆   ◆   ◆

The Amazon River basin provides the world with 40 percent of its oxygen and with 25 percent of all the fresh water in the world. Of the 22,000 known species of plants, over 18,000 are found in the Amazon region; also, over 80 percent of all the known species of freshwater fish live in its waters.

◆   ◆   ◆   ◆   ◆

When Krakatoa, an Indonesian island, erupted in 1883, debris fell as far away as Madagascar, the sound was heard in Texas and the effects of the tidal waves were observable in the English Channel.

◆ ◆ ◆ ◆ ◆

According to criminologists, the odds of finding two sets of fingerprints exactly alike are about one in a *billion trillon*. A duplicate set has never been found.

◆ ◆ ◆ ◆ ◆

A university study has concluded that it must be fun to be stupid. According to their findings, stupid people laugh far more than smart people; the amount of laughter is in inverse proportion to a person's intelligence.

◆ ◆ ◆ ◆ ◆

The yo-yo was originally a deadly Filipino weapon until it was adapted and introduced as a toy in 1929.

◆ ◆ ◆ ◆ ◆

American golf balls are slightly larger than the official British and Canadian golf balls.

◆ ◆ ◆ ◆ ◆

Castor oil is used as the liquid center of many brands of golf balls.

◆ ◆ ◆ ◆ ◆

The nation of Costa Rica has no standing army. Reports were that occasionally when an important head of state visited, the government borrowed a cannon from El Salvador for a military salute.

◆ ◆ ◆ ◆ ◆

As many people know, the White House was originally gray stone. The building was painted white after it was burned by the British in 1814 and the walls became blackened by smoke.

The interesting and little-known thing is that the White House was called the "White House" several years *before* it was painted white.

♦   ♦   ♦   ♦   ♦

The American Presidents Washington, Lincoln, Adams and Monroe were all descendants of King Edward I of England. Presidents Jefferson, Taft and Grant were direct descendants of Scotland's King David I. In all, thirteen American Presidents have had royal blood.

♦   ♦   ♦   ♦   ♦

Throughout the civilized world, there have been only 233 years of peace since 1496 B.C.

♦   ♦   ♦   ♦   ♦

◆ 10 ◆
ONE WAY TO DO IT

An ancient remedy for toothache was to eat a mouse.

◆   ◆   ◆   ◆   ◆

You can tell what time it is merely by looking at a flower. Many flowers open at different times of the day. Morning glories open between 5 and 6 A.M.; daisies between 8 and 9, and tulips between 10 and 11.

Cow Facts

In ancient Carthage, people thought that they could cure indigestion by placing a cow's tail on their stomach.

◆　◆　◆　◆　◆

A cow's moo was once a unit of distance in India. It was based upon the distance that the sound of a cow's moo would carry.

◆　◆　◆　◆　◆

It is possible to make a positive identification of a cow by taking a "fingerprint" of its nose.

It takes three people to artificially inseminate a whooping crane.

◆　◆　◆　◆　◆

The economy of the Pacific island of Nauru, which has a population of 6,056 and one of the world's highest per capita incomes, is based almost entirely on bird droppings. The bird droppings are exported as fertilizer, adding vasts sums of money to the gross national product of the tiny country.

◆　◆　◆　◆　◆

If you measure the distance around an elephant's foot and double it, you will find out its approximate height.

◆　◆　◆　◆　◆

Studies show that the best time to teach an earthworm tricks is shortly before midnight.

◆　◆　◆　◆　◆

According to a study by researchers at Colgate University, students would do better on tests if they were allowed to take them while lying on the floor. The study discovered that a horizontal position with feet slightly raised enabled the students to solve math problems 7.4 percent faster and with 14 percent greater accuracy.

◆　◆　◆　◆　◆

Prisoners in Paris' infamous fortress, the Bastille, were each given three bottles of wine to drink every day. This kept them in such a state of mellow inebriation that they were virtually incapable of escaping.

◆　◆　◆　◆　◆

Instead of wearing a watch, George Washington often carried around a small sundial.

◆　◆　◆　◆　◆

Although William Seward, the famous American Secretary of State during the Lincoln administration, was a diminutive man, the statue of him in New York City depicts him as being 6 feet 4 inches tall. Actually, the statue was originally intended to be that of Lincoln. When the contract for the Lincoln statute was cancelled at the last minute, the sculptor resourcefully welded a new head (Seward's) onto Lincoln's gangly body.

◆　◆　◆　◆　◆

The famous firm of Thomas Cook Ltd. provided the travel arrangements for the Battle of Khartoum. The government felt that the company was far better equipped to plan the campaign than the army was. The project involved transportating 18,000 men, 130,000 tons of supplies aboard at least 28 chartered ships, 6,000 railway cars and 650 boats from England up the Nile to Khartoum. Although the army failed to succeed in its mission, Thomas Cook Ltd. provided all the services agreed upon in the contract and completed the mission on the specified date.

◆　◆　◆　◆　◆

Loser?

When he was 22, he failed in business. When he was 23, he ran for the legislature and lost. When he was 24, he failed in business again. The following year he was elected to the legislature. When he was 26, his sweetheart died. At the age of 27, he had a nervous breakdown. When he was 29, he was defeated for the post of Speaker of the House in the State Legislature. When he was 31, he was defeated as Elector. When he was 34, he ran for Congress and lost. At the age of 37, he ran for Congress and finally won. Two years later, he ran again and lost his seat in Congress. At the age of 46, he ran for the U.S. Senate and lost. The following year he ran for Vice President and lost that, too. He ran for the Senate again and again lost. Finally, at the age of 51, he was elected President of the United States. Who was this perpetual "loser"? Abraham Lincoln.

Julius Caesar always wore a laurel wreath on his head because he wanted to hide the fact that he was bald.

♦　♦　♦　♦　♦

Czar Paul I of Russia became so irritated over people making jokes about his baldness that he issued a decree stating that anyone who mentioned the subject in his presence would be subject to the penalty of death by flogging.

♦　♦　♦　♦　♦

The state of Maine is the world's largest producer of toothpicks. Each year Maine manufactures over 26,000,000,000 toothpicks, which, if placed end to end, would reach to the moon and back three times or encircle the earth at the equator 60 times.

It is possible to have a fingernail transplant.

◆   ◆   ◆   ◆   ◆

Gregor Mendel was the Austrian monk whose experiments with garden peas proved the basic laws of heredity. Although he was right, modern scientists contend that he must have faked some of his experiments and doctored his data.

The problem is that Mendel's plants, if you believe his figures, seemed to grow *precisely* according to the laws of heredity he developed. The late British statistician, Sir Ronald Fisher, has calculated that the odds are 10,000 to one that Mendel's figures were faked.

◆   ◆   ◆   ◆   ◆

Some pundits date the beginning of the end of communism to the installation of the first pay toilet in the history of Moscow on Prospect Marx, not far from Red Square, in 1987.

◆   ◆   ◆   ◆   ◆

Victor Hugo's classic novel, *Les Miserables,* caused a sensation when it was first published in installments in France in 1862. After the first volume came out, the author was anxious to know how it was selling. He sent the publisher a telegram that simply said: "?" The publisher, equally thrifty, wired back: "!"

◆   ◆   ◆   ◆   ◆

WHAT'S IN A NAME?

Charles III, better known as Charles the Simple, had claim to the throne of France through his grandfather, who was known as Charles the Bald, and first exercised this claim when Charles the Fat was overthrown in 887. Incidentally, aside from Charles the Fat, Charles the Bald and Charles the Simple, there have also been kings known as Charles the Mad, Charles the Lame and Charles the Bad.

♦ ♦ ♦ ♦ ♦

Aviator-hero Charles Lindbergh's family name was not originally Lindbergh. His grandfather fled to America from Europe to escape charges because of his unorthodox political views. If his ancestor had not changed the family name, this great American hero would have been born Charles Mannson, and shared that name with Charles Manson, the notorious American cult murderer.

◆ ◆ ◆ ◆ ◆

Boca Raton, an exclusive enclave in Florida, is synonymous with wealth and power. People pay outrageous sums of money to buy a home that has a Boca Raton address. Ironically, the name of this wealthy and desirable community is Spanish for "the mouse's mouth."

◆ ◆ ◆ ◆ ◆

When Our Lady of Guadalupe Church in the French Quarter of New Orleans was being restored in the 1920's, workmen received a statue of a saint from Italy. There was no identification on the statue or the crate it came in except for the address and the Italian phrase, "e sepdito" (meaning "expedite" or "rush").

The workmen assumed that this was the name of the saint and it was installed as such. The statue has borne the name of an Italian postal marking ever since, and the priest at the church has no idea what the name of the saint really is.

◆ ◆ ◆ ◆ ◆

The nation of El Salvador became so annoyed with people mistakenly calling it San Salvador or just plain Salvador that for a time it refused to accept government dispatches that had the name wrong on the address.

◆ ◆ ◆ ◆ ◆

It would seem a sure bet for a theatrical producer to invest in a Broadway show titled *Sweet Charity*, *South Pacific*, *The Boy Friend* or *Carnival*, wouldn't it? After all, they were all enormous hits on Broadway.

However, an investor had better check the fine print on his contract, because there have been a total of *ten* legitimate Broadway shows that shared those titles. Six of them, including three separate plays entitled *Carnival*, were disastrous flops.

◆ ◆ ◆ ◆ ◆

The title of the song "A Frog Went a'Courting" comes from Queen Elizabeth's habit of giving her suitors amusing animal nicknames. Sir Walter Raleigh was referred to as "the fish" and the French ambassador as "the ape." Her would-be suitor, the Duc d'Alençon, was called "the frog," and his efforts to win the Queen's attentions are immortalized in the tune, "A Frog Went a'Courting."

◆ ◆ ◆ ◆ ◆

On February 1, 1887, just before leaving for the city land office to register his new 120-acre land acquisition, Los Angeles real estate entrepreneur Harvey Wilcox asked his wife, Daeida, what name he should give to his new real estate venture.

She thought for a moment and remembered "Hollywood," the name of the summer cottage of a total stranger she'd once chatted with on a train.

No one knows who the stranger was or has the slightest idea where the original cottage that gave us the name "Hollywood" was located.

◆ ◆ ◆ ◆ ◆

In the movies based on Ian Fleming's series of thrillers, secret agent James Bond is anything but a saint. There is, however, a church in Toronto called the St. James Bond United Church.

The church got is unusual name when the St. James Square Presbyterian Church and the Bond Street Congregational Church merged several decades ago.

At the time, the elders of the churches couldn't have known that the name James Bond was destined later to become deeply associated with worldly matters.

◆ ◆ ◆ ◆ ◆

English last names were not generally adopted until the 13th century, or later. People were called by their first name and sometimes further identified by their profession or where they lived. If their children had a different profession or lived in a different place, they generally were known by a different "last name."

◆ ◆ ◆ ◆ ◆

The name of Sabena, the Belgian airline, is the shortened form of the company's original name, "Societie Anonyme Belge pour l'exploitation de la Navigation Aerinne."

◆ ◆ ◆ ◆ ◆

Have you ever called anyone an imbecile? An imbecile, according to the medical definition of the word, is more intelligent than an idiot but less intelligent than a moron.

◆ ◆ ◆ ◆ ◆

Scientists in Bangor, Wales, have invented an electronic beeper that can be attached to sheep so that the shepherd can follow their wanderings without having to leave home. They call the thing a Bangor Orange Position Estimating Equipment for Pastures, or BO PEEP for short.

◆ ◆ ◆ ◆ ◆

The great American naval hero, John Paul Jones, was not really named John Paul Jones. He was born John Paul in Scotland in 1747. He changed his name to John Paul Jones in 1773 when he fled to America to escape his *second* murder charge.

◆ ◆ ◆ ◆ ◆

Brazil holds the distinction of being the world's only nation named after a nut. The Portuguese named the region after a family of dyewood trees they found there, the most famous of which is the Brazil nut tree.

◆   ◆   ◆   ◆   ◆

The dogwood got its name because people used the tree to make a homemade flea remedy for their dogs.

◆   ◆   ◆   ◆   ◆

Three Points Cape in the Gulf of Guinea off West Africa has the unusual nickname, "The Land Nearest Nowhere," where zero latitude meets zero longitude at zero altitude.

◆   ◆   ◆   ◆   ◆

The famous American Indian princess, Pocahontas, was not really named Pocahontas. Her real name was Matoaka. However, she was such a precocious child that she earned the nickname Pocahontas, meaning "the playful one." When she married Captain John Smith, she was given the English name "Rebecca."

◆   ◆   ◆   ◆   ◆

Mr. Jesse James, who shared his name with a famous Wild West train robber, served as a state official in Texas for 36 years. His position? State treasurer.

◆   ◆   ◆   ◆   ◆

— ◆ 12 ◆ —

GOOD THINKING!

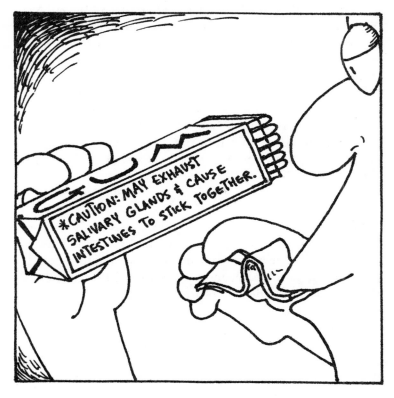

In the 1890s an American doctor published a treatise warning that chewing gum would "exhaust the salivary glands and cause the intestines to stick together."

◆　◆　◆　◆　◆

In colonial Virginia, it was considered treason to conspire to damage or destroy a tobacco plant. The law carried with it the death penalty for offenders.

During the same period, smoking was a crime punishable by death in both the Mogul empire and in Czarist Russia.

♦   ♦   ♦   ♦   ♦

Lawrence E. Wallick was arrested in Ocean Beach, New York, on charges of eating a chocolate chip cookie in public. The resort town had an anti-littering ordinance that banned eating in public or carrying open containers of food. Tried along with Mr. Wallick was Ruth Bushnell, who was accused of eating crumb cake and Michael Mastandrea, who was allegedly seen holding a glass of water.

Although it may have been illegal to eat such foods as pizza and hot dogs in public in Ocean Beach, the right to eat an ice cream cone in public was always protected by the law.

♦   ♦   ♦   ♦   ♦

When the English poet Lord Byron was at Cambridge, the university had a regulation against students keeping dogs or cats. Byron got around this rule against pets by purchasing a trained bear, arguing that although the university rule prohibited dogs and cats, it did not specifically outlaw pet bears.

♦   ♦   ♦   ♦   ♦

According to the ancient code of Hammurabi, the early Babylonian legal code, it was proper to put your wife up as collateral for a loan. If you didn't repay the loan, the creditor could seize your wife. The code stipulated, however, that the creditor could only keep her for three years and that he was required to return her in as good condition as she was when she came.

♦   ♦   ♦   ♦   ♦

According to a law in Berea, Ohio, dogs and cats out after dark were required to wear a taillight.

♦   ♦   ♦   ♦   ♦

According to the law in Pocatello, Idaho, it is illegal to look unhappy.

Under Arrest

A number of horses facing execution in a federal drive to reduce the overpopulation of wild horses in the American West have been sentenced to prison instead. The animals have been acquired by the Idaho State Penitentiary.

◆ ◆ ◆ ◆ ◆

A Wellington, New Zealand, cow was sentenced to two days in jail for eating the grass in front of the city courthouse.

When his pilot's license was revoked, a Canadian man became so angry that he took off in his plane and "bombed" Calgary, Alberta, with one hundred pounds of pig manure.

◆ ◆ ◆ ◆ ◆

In the late 1960's a Texas legislator became annoyed with his colleagues' habit of passing bills without giving them proper study and consideration. He therefore introduced a bill commending "Mr. Albert DiSalvo for his outstanding work in population control." At the time, Mr. DiSalvo was on trial for a series of murders and was better known by his grisly nickname "The Boston Strangler." The bill passed unanimously.

◆ ◆ ◆ ◆ ◆

The U.S. Senate once passed a resolution requiring the Senate dining room to serve bean soup every day.

◆ ◆ ◆ ◆ ◆

Great Britain's Houses of Parliament were built on the banks of the Thames following the advice of the Duke of Wellington, who thought they should be placed where a mob couldn't surround them.

♦ ♦ ♦ ♦ ♦

Industrialist Henry Ford once attempted to buy the Eiffel Tower and have it shipped to the United States.

♦ ♦ ♦ ♦ ♦

One of the earliest and cleverest uses of psychological warfare was thought up by Alexander the Great in 328 B.C. During his campaign to conquer India, he ordered his blacksmiths to make helmets, bridles and pieces of armor that were many sizes too large for any of his soldiers. He then deliberately left them behind where the enemy leaders would be certain to find them. The leaders and soldiers were terrified and demoralized when they saw the size of the armor that they thought belonged to Alexander's horses and men.

♦ ♦ ♦ ♦ ♦

During World War II, the Germans provided their left-handed soldiers with weapons that were specifically designed for them.

♦ ♦ ♦ ♦ ♦

The citizens of the town of Quayaquil, Ecuador, decided to erect a statue of the great Ecuadorian poet Jose Olmedo in the town square. They were dismayed, however, when they found out how much it would cost to commission the statue. The problem was solved when the foundry offered them a second-hand statue of Lord Byron cheap. They bought the statue of Byron, erected it in the square and put Jose Olmedo's name on the pedestal.

♦ ♦ ♦ ♦ ♦

A marketing survey conducted for corporations attempting to cash in on the counter-culture of the 1960's concluded—among other things—that people who opposed the Vietnam war tended to buy Roquefort cheese and avoid Minute Rice.

♦ ♦ ♦ ♦ ♦

During the Middle Ages, 115 of the 365 days of the year were religious holidays.

♦ ♦ ♦ ♦ ♦

An American doctor has attempted removing warts through hypnosis. In an experiment carried out by Dr. Hilton V. Kline, president of the Society for Chemical and Experimental Hypnosis, the patient was placed in a trance and told to picture the warts falling off. It worked (or so he claims).

♦ ♦ ♦ ♦ ♦

Among the organizations that you can join around the world according to *Spectator*, a magazine published by the Chrysler Corporation, are: The International Footprint Association, The Dairy Goat Council of America, The Oyster Shell Institute, National Prune Juice Packers Association, God's Garden Club (a church in Los Angeles), The Forum for Cosmic Truth (based on Staten Island, of all places), The National Indignation Society, Simandl-Bruderschaft ("brotherhood of hen-pecked husbands," Krems, Germany), Society for the Prevention of Calling Sleeping-Car Porters George (members have included song-writer George M. Cohan and French statesman Georges Clemenceau), National Association for the Prevention of the Practice of Referring to a Bathroom as a John, The Bible and Fruit Mission and The "What Good Are We?" Club (located appropriately enough, in Washington, D.C.).

♦ ♦ ♦ ♦ ♦

The great chef and cookbook writer, James Beard, once said, if he were forced to practice cannibalism, "I might manage if there were enough tarragon around."

♦   ♦   ♦   ♦   ♦

George Bernard Shaw had a tiny eight-foot-square writing hut built on wheels so that he could rotate it by hand to follow the sun all day long.

♦   ♦   ♦   ♦   ♦

Thomas Jefferson is credited with inventing the coat hanger.

♦   ♦   ♦   ♦   ♦

Scientists believe that human beings developed the ski in the Paleolithic era of the Stone Age—about the same time they learned the secret of fire.

♦   ♦   ♦   ♦   ♦

The U.S. Secretary of Agriculture protested the removal of a plaque dedicating the Agriculture Department's cafeteria to the Wild West guide, Alferd Packer. The Secretary asserted that the late Mr. Packer "exemplifies the spirit and the fare of this Agriculture Department cafeteria."

Why was the plaque being removed? Alferd Parker was convicted in 1874 on charges of killing and eating five Colorado prospectors.

♦   ♦   ♦   ♦   ♦

The U.S. Army accidentally ordered an 82-year supply of freeze-dried tuna salad mix for its troops in Europe.

♦   ♦   ♦   ♦   ♦

Mrs. Elizabeth Adams sued the Holy Sepulchre Cemetery in East Orange, New Jersey, for injuries she suffered when a 600-pound tombstone toppled over onto her foot.

This was not the first grave tragedy that had befallen the Adams family, who apparently do not believe in cremation. Twenty years ago, Mrs. Adams' nephew was squashed to death by a tombstone.

◆　◆　◆　◆　◆

Rather than hire a demolition company, a St. Petersburg, Florida woman hired a karate school to tear down her old garage. Five students kicked the garage into a neat pile of kindling wood in a matter of hours.

◆　◆　◆　◆　◆

Anne Nichols' 1922 play, *Abie's Irish Rose*, was rejected by so many producers that the author decided to produce it herself. It had a run of 2,327 performances, a record that was not broken for several decades.

◆　◆　◆　◆　◆

As a young draftee at Camp Upton, in Yaphank, New York, in 1917, Irving Berlin wrote an all-soldier musical revue called *Yip, Yip, Yaphank*. Twenty years later he dusted off a tune that he had cut from the show, and wrote new lyrics.

The song that had lain abandoned for two decades? "God Bless America."

◆　◆　◆　◆　◆

In a two-year study of 400 students at Simon Fraser University in Vancouver, British Columbia, sociologist Herbert Adams attempted to determine the ability of well-educated college students to identify well-known people in history.

In the multiple choice test he administered, a *majority* of the students identified the Nazi criminal, Adolf Eichmann as "an aide of former President Nixon," apparently confusing him with Nixon aide, John Ehrlichman. A sizable minority identified the French philosopher Jean-Jacques

Rousseau as "a famous deep-sea diver who makes television specials."

♦   ♦   ♦   ♦   ♦

An experiment conducted for an American psychology magazine, concluded, among other things, that test subjects who believed that they had given a confederate painful electrical shocks were more willing to help save California redwood trees. The conclusion of the study was that much charitable behavior is motivated by guilt or shame.

♦   ♦   ♦   ♦   ♦

A university in Florida has a sign posted in the restroom next to a multi-million dollar experimental nuclear reactor that reads "Please do not flush the toilet while the reactor is running."

It seems that flushing the toilet seriously reduces the water pressure in the reactor's cooling system. University officials claim that this design problem is not dangerous.

♦   ♦   ♦   ♦   ♦

◆ 13 ◆

WHY IT'S BETTER TO BE AN ANIMAL THAN A PERSON

Members of the Junag tribe in India build comfortable thatched houses on stilts. However, the houses are for the use of their *goats*. The people sleep in the open air underneath their houses.

◆　◆　◆　◆　◆

Dogs are far better at finding gas leaks than any instrument scientists have ever been able to invent.

♦   ♦   ♦   ♦   ♦

The Pekingese was once held sacred in the Orient and no one outside the Emperor's court was allowed to own one. In ancient China, the "dog-napping" of a Pekingese was a crime punishable by death.

♦   ♦   ♦   ♦   ♦

Although it is a large and ungainly creature when it is on the ground, in the air the wild turkey is capable of flying at speeds of 55 miles per hour.

♦   ♦   ♦   ♦   ♦

The breed of flea that inhabits humans is capable of broad-jumping 13 feet. Its rate of acceleration is approximately thirty times that which a human being can withstand without losing consciousness.

♦   ♦   ♦   ♦   ♦

When a cockroach is in a hurry, it rears up on its hind legs to run. Scientists have calculated that if a cockroach were the size of a man it could reach speeds of over 200 miles per hour.

♦   ♦   ♦   ♦   ♦

There are 15,000 different species of flies found in North America.

♦   ♦   ♦   ♦   ♦

Caterpillars have more than 2,000 muscles in their bodies. Humans have fewer than 700.

♦   ♦   ♦   ♦   ♦

A full-grown adult rat has a body that is so flexible he can squeeze through a hole less than one inch around. He can also gnaw through cinder blocks, fall five stories onto concrete and scurry away unhurt and swim for three days without resting. Rats are also capable of multiplying so rapidly that in a year and a half a single pair could have one million descendants.

◆   ◆   ◆   ◆   ◆

According to the laws of California, it's illegal to set a mousetrap without first obtaining a hunting license.

◆   ◆   ◆   ◆   ◆

The singing house mouse has a vocal range of about two octaves, far better than the average human being. Theoretically, at least, it would be able to sing the aria Sempre Libera, from "La Traviata,"—if it knew the words.

◆   ◆   ◆   ◆   ◆

In the animal kingdom, the dormouse holds the record for sleeping. It spends almost half a year in hibernation.

◆   ◆   ◆   ◆   ◆

The tiny animal, the shrew, probably holds the eating record among mammals. It eats over three times its weight in food every day. If a 150-pound man ate like that, he would have to devour over 450 pounds of food every day.

◆   ◆   ◆   ◆   ◆

An adult opossum weighs about 28,000 times its weight at birth. If human beings grew at the same rate, each of us would weigh at least 200,000 pounds.

◆   ◆   ◆   ◆   ◆

The Alaskan brown bear is the largest meat-eating mammal that lives on land. However, the offspring of bears are smaller in proportion to the size of the parent than the offspring of any other mammal, except for pouched animals such as the opossum. Although a 120-pound woman is likely to give birth to a 6-8 pound baby, a 600-pound bear might have a cub that weighs a mere 8-10 ounces.

◆　◆　◆　◆　◆

The awkward-looking polar bear is capable of out-running a reindeer. It can reach speeds of 25 miles per hour for fairly extended distances. In water, it is quite possible that it could outswim an Olympic swimmer.

◆　◆　◆　◆　◆

The grey wolf can reach speeds of 35 miles per hour and clear 16 feet at a single bound. It can run at a speed of 20 miles per hour for hours on end, thereby wearing out even the swiftest prey.

◆　◆　◆　◆　◆

A python can go for as long as a year without eating.

◆　◆　◆　◆　◆

Most breeds of minnows are very tiny. However, one member of the minnow family, the giant Siamese minnow, can reach lengths of over eight feet and weigh as much as 300 pounds.

◆　◆　◆　◆　◆

A catfish can "taste" its prey through sense organs in its tail.

◆　◆　◆　◆　◆

A whale's mating call can be heard 100 miles away.

◆　◆　◆　◆　◆

◆ 14 ◆
WHY THINGS ARE
THE WAY THEY ARE

The St. Bernard rescue dogs are often depicted with a small keg of brandy around their necks. Actually, the dogs do not wear a cask and never have. St. Bernards have been used to rescue stranded travellers since the early 1600's. During the 1800's, Sir Edwin Landseer, an artist who was famous as a painter of animals, did a series of illustrations depicting St. Bernards wearing brandy casks. Ever since then, people have assumed that the famous rescue dogs have little kegs around their necks. They don't.

♦ ♦ ♦ ♦ ♦

The modern typewriter keyboard was deliberately designed to be as inconvenient as possible. On earlier models of the typewriter, the keyboard was arranged so that the most common letters in the English language were located in the middle row. Typists soon became so quick that they continually jammed the primitive machines. The inventor solved the problem by scrambling the letters on the keyboard and creating a deliberately inconvenient arrangement. This slowed down the typists and thus prevented them from accidentally jamming the typewriter. Although modern typewriters are virtually jam-proof, they still have the deliberately inefficient keyboard arrangement designed for the first primitive typing machines.

♦ ♦ ♦ ♦ ♦

Have you ever noticed that on a clock with Roman numerals one of the numbers is not written with a standard Roman numeral? The four is usually written with a IIII rather than a IV. The reason is to provide visual balance with the VIII on the opposite side of the dial.

♦ ♦ ♦ ♦ ♦

Why do the New York Yankees wear pinstriped uniforms? Simple. It's because Babe Ruth was fat. The owner of the Yankees thought that maybe stripes on the uniform would make his star player look thinner. The legacy of Babe Ruth's pot belly continues on in the famous pinstripes of the great New York team.

♦ ♦ ♦ ♦ ♦

The palms of your hands and the soles of your feet wrinkle after long submersion in water because they have no fat-secreting glands. Areas of the skin that lack glands that secrete sebum, a fatty lubricant substance, tend to absorb water, swell and wrinkle.

◆   ◆   ◆   ◆   ◆

In early Roman times, the calendar year ended on February 30th and the next year began on March 1st. During his reign, Julius Caesar renamed the month of Quintilius—the month in which he was born—in his own honor, giving us the month named July. Since July had only 30 days at that time, Julius eliminated the last day of the Roman calendar year (February 30th) and added one day to July so that it would not be shorter than any of the other months.

Later, Augustus Caesar decided to rename the month Sextilius after himself, giving us the month named August. Up to that point August had only 30 days. Since Augustus didn't want *his* month to be shorter than the month named after Julius Caesar, he took another day off the end of the Roman calendar year (February 29th) and gave August 31 days.

◆   ◆   ◆   ◆   ◆

The charming children's nonsense rhyme "Ring Around the Rosie" actually refers to the Black Death, which killed 25,000,000 people during the 14th century. The word "rosie" refers to the reddish patches that appeared on the skin of people who had the plague. People carried around "A pocket full of posies," or other sweet-smelling flowers and herbs, hoping that the sweet odors would ward off the "evil vapors" of the plague. The line "They all fall down," of course, really means "fall down dead." Fully a quarter of the population of Europe was wiped out by the Black Death.

◆   ◆   ◆   ◆   ◆

The customs of covering your mouth when you yawn and of saying "God bless you" when someone else sneezes are both rooted in ancient superstitions. Primitive people believed that yawning gave evil spirits an opportunity to enter their bodies. To prevent this they clapped their hands over their mouths when they yawned so that evil spirits wouldn't get in.

Ancient people also believed that when you sneeze your soul somehow momentarily escapes from your body. People said "God bless you" in order to restore God's grace and protection to the person who sneezed. The custom was further encouraged during the Middle Ages. One of the early symptoms of the Black Death was that victims had sneezing fits. People in danger of death obviously needed all of God's blessings.

♦　♦　♦　♦　♦

Ever notice that an elephant's tusks never seem to be of equal length? It's because elephants, like humans, fish, birds and insects, are either "left-handed" or "right-handed". A "left-handed" elephant tends to use his left tusk more, so the tusk wears down faster.

♦　♦　♦　♦　♦

KNOCKING AT DEATH'S DOOR

The great Greek writer Aeschylus is said to have been killed when an eagle dropped a tortoise on his head.

♦   ♦   ♦   ♦   ♦

William Shakespeare, England's greatest writer, and Miguel de Cervantes, Spain's greatest writer, both died on April 23, 1616.

♦   ♦   ♦   ♦   ♦

The popular American songwriter Stephen Foster was born on the day that Thomas Jefferson and John Adams both died, July 4th, 1826, the 50th anniversary of the signing of the Declaration of Independence.

◆ ◆ ◆ ◆ ◆

One fascinating but absolutely useless fact about Thomas Edison is that his friend Henry Ford is said to have kept Edison's dying breath in a bottle.

◆ ◆ ◆ ◆ ◆

The English writer Ben Jonson has the unusual distinction of being the only man in Westminster Abbey to be buried standing up. A number of years before he died, Jonson had selected the exact spot where he wanted to be interred in the Abbey. Upon his death, however, it was discovered that the spot was already occupied except for a space that was barely eighteen inches square. According to legend, the great author was stuffed into the grave in a sitting or crouching position.

◆ ◆ ◆ ◆ ◆

Marfan's Syndrome is a hereditary disease that causes elongation of the limbs during youth and frequently results in terminal heart disease during adulthood. In the early 1970's, a patient with Marfan's Syndrome casually mentioned to his doctor that he was related to Abraham Lincoln. Intrigued, the doctor did some extensive historical research into Lincoln's health. He concluded that Lincoln had Marfan's Syndrome and that, if he had not been assassinated, he would have died of natural causes within a matter of months.

◆ ◆ ◆ ◆ ◆

When Abraham Lincoln was shot by John Wilkes Booth at Ford's Theater, he was carried across the street to a roominghouse, where he died in a small first-floor room.

Later, it was discovered that an actor friend of Booth's had been a previous tenant of the room and that Booth himself had taken afternoon naps in the very bed that Lincoln later died in.

◆ ◆ ◆ ◆ ◆

In Egypt, cats were held sacred. When Egyptian cats died, their owners were expected to shave off their eyebrows as a sign of mourning.

◆ ◆ ◆ ◆ ◆

In ancient Egypt, cats were often buried in bronze coffins in special mausoleums complete with mummified mice for the afterlife.

◆ ◆ ◆ ◆ ◆

The Hungarian actor, Bela Lugosi, created his version of Dracula on stage in the 1920's. His 1930 film depiction of the character was so vivid and chilling that he was typecast in similar roles in low-budget, poor-quality horror movies for the rest of his career. When he died in 1956, he was buried in the Dracula cape he had made so famous almost three decades before.

◆ ◆ ◆ ◆ ◆

Until the early 19th century, burning at the stake was a legal form of execution in many parts of the United States.

◆ ◆ ◆ ◆ ◆

During the Middle Ages, there were dozens of murder trials against animals. The records of at least 90 such trials have survived, the first against a pig in 1266 and the last against a horse in 1692.

A large majority of the cases involved pigs who had killed small children. Children were kept away from large dangerous animals such as horses and bulls, but careless parents often let them play near the pigs. The legal procedure was virtually the same as for a human defendant. Sometimes the pig was tortured and its squeals were recorded as a confession of guilt. It was kept in solitary confinement in jail and put under guard as if it were a human criminal. During the trial, the court sometimes provided it with a defense lawyer. The execution was carried out as if the doomed animal were a man. Sometimes the pig's nose was cut off and a human mask was placed over its mutilated snout; on some occasions, they went so far as to dress up the animal in a man's waistcoat and breeches before they led him to the gallows.

◆ ◆ ◆ ◆ ◆

During a month long doctors' strike in Israel, the death rate *declined* by 50 percent.

◆ ◆ ◆ ◆ ◆

◆ 16 ◆
INTIMATE DETAILS

When a male fish begins blowing bubbles in his aquarium, it means he's ready for breeding.

◆ ◆ ◆ ◆ ◆

Five-star general Dwight David Eisenhower owned a specially-made pair of pajamas with five stars on the lapels.

◆ ◆ ◆ ◆ ◆

The modern padded bra was invented by Englishman D. J. Kennedy as a safety device for women athletes. Mr. Kennedy learned that women competitors at the 1928 Olympics had often suffered painful bruises on their bosoms during their athletic endeavors. He immediately set to work on a padded garment that would protect the ladies' breasts from harm. His invention inspired the French dress designer De Brassiere to add padding to the new undergarment he was then popularizing.

◆   ◆   ◆   ◆   ◆

The advance team of American workers in China who prepared President Nixon's historic trip to Red China in 1970 developed a mysterious rash on their buttocks. Full-color photographs of the afflicted areas were rushed to Washington for analysis. The rash was diagnosed as poison sumac caused by the wood used in making Chinese toilet seats. Security agents carefully checked dozens of toilet seats to be sure that the American President would not be struck down with the affliction.

◆   ◆   ◆   ◆   ◆

Historians believe that one of the main reasons the French lost at Waterloo was that, at the time of the battle, Napoleon was bedridden with a terrible case of hemorrhoids.

◆   ◆   ◆   ◆   ◆

Left-handed people tend to scratch themselves with their right hand while right-handed people tend to scratch with their left.

◆   ◆   ◆   ◆   ◆

Anne Boleyn, the second wife of Henry VIII, had six fingers on one hand.

◆   ◆   ◆   ◆   ◆

Studies at the University of Virginia suggest that you are more likely to catch a cold by holding hands than by kissing. Tests showed that forty percent of the subjects carried traces of common cold viruses on their hands, but only eight percent carried viruses on their lips or mouth.

♦ ♦ ♦ ♦ ♦

A researcher at Lake Forest College in Illinois has concluded that dark-eyed people are more strongly stimulated by violence, rough language and provocative pictures than blue-eyed people. The test subjects were connected to instruments that measured their respiration, pulse and other factors while they were exposed to various photographic and tape recordings. The tests showed that dark-eyed women reacted most strongly, followed by blue-eyed women, dark-eyed men and finally blue-eyed men.

♦ ♦ ♦ ♦ ♦

Queen Elizabeth I of England wore horn rim glasses, had false teeth and was totally bald.

♦ ♦ ♦ ♦ ♦

During his entire life, King Louis XIV of France only took *three* baths, and *none* of them willingly. The first "bath" was when he was baptized by immersion; the second was when one of his mistresses insisted that he wash himself; and the third was when he had to soak in a tub of water after his doctor lanced a sore on his *derrière*.

♦ ♦ ♦ ♦ ♦

It is illegal to leave a naked dummy in a store window in New York City.

♦ ♦ ♦ ♦ ♦

An archbishop of Manila was named Cardinal Sin.

♦ ♦ ♦ ♦ ♦

A polar bear can smell you 20 miles away.

U.S. Scientific Research

The National Science Foundation spent $53,000 on a study on the sex life of snails.

◆ ◆ ◆ ◆ ◆

The Natural Science Foundation spent $132,500 on a study to determine "Why people fall in love."

◆ ◆ ◆ ◆ ◆

The U.S. government spent $57,800 on a study that consisted entirely of measuring the physical dimensions of airline stewardesses.

◆ ◆ ◆ ◆ ◆

According to careful measurement taken by teams of medical experts during an American medical research project, people who live in cities have longer, thicker and denser hair in their noses than people who live in the countryside.

The kiss did not become widespread in Western society until about 500 A.D. It was popularized by the Romans and slowly spread through the various Western cultures. There are still many countries, such as Japan and China, where people do not generally kiss. The Eskimos and the Polynesians greet one another by rubbing noses, while the Samoans simply smell each other.

◆ ◆ ◆ ◆ ◆

Only male canaries sing.

◆ ◆ ◆ ◆ ◆

Queen Victoria is said to have worn a brand-new pair of bloomers every day of her long lifetime. Although it would seem that this glut of bloomers would tend to decrease the value of these artifacts on the auction market, there is a thriving business in Victoria's "unmentionables." At recent auctions, they have fetched as much as $280.

◆　◆　◆　◆　◆

In Minnesota, it is illegal to hang men's and women's undergarments on the same clothesline.

◆　◆　◆　◆　◆

In ancient Greece, soldiers often went into battle totally naked from the waist down.

◆　◆　◆　◆　◆

One reason that the operas of Handel are rarely performed now is that there is a severe shortage of eunuchs in the musical world today. Many of Handel's operatic parts were written for castrati.

◆　◆　◆　◆　◆

Female giraffes are so disinterested in sex that they occasionally just walk away during the sex act, allowing the male to crash to the ground.

◆　◆　◆　◆　◆

When you blush, your stomach lining becomes redder; when your face turns white, your stomach becomes paler.

◆　◆　◆　◆　◆

Ah, love! A newly-married couple in Rotterdam, New York, had their first marital spat on the way home from their wedding reception. When the husband got out of the car, his new wife gunned the engine and ran over him, killing him instantly.

◆　◆　◆　◆　◆

The great British Prime Minister Winston Churchill once proposed marriage to actress Ethel Barrymore. She turned him down.

♦   ♦   ♦   ♦   ♦

Writer and diplomat Claire Boothe Luce added the "e" to the name Booth to cover up her familial relationship to John Wilkes Booth, the man who assassinated Abraham Lincoln.

♦   ♦   ♦   ♦   ♦

The British government funded a study that involved secretly photographing people sitting on experimental toilet seats.

♦   ♦   ♦   ♦   ♦

A study at the University of Iowa has discovered that looking at nude people can stop you from coughing.

♦   ♦   ♦   ♦   ♦

◆ 17 ◆

THE STORY BEHIND THE STORY

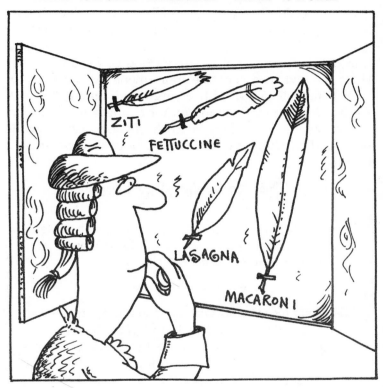

Most music historians believe that the line in "Yankee Doodle" ("he stuck a feather in his hat and called it macaroni") refers to a hat that was worn by Oliver Cromwell. Cromwell was particularly fond of wearing an odd Italian hat with a long feather called a macaroni. The lyrics of the song were written to ridicule Cromwell and his ridiculous headgear. One hundred years later, the song was used to ridicule the American colonists. However, the Americans loved the song, and it became virtually the theme song of the American Revolution. Oddly enough, some of the most popular lyrics were written by a man who served in the British army.

♦ ♦ ♦ ♦ ♦

In London there is a statue of King Charles II on horseback trampling his enemy, Oliver Cromwell, underfoot. Actually the statue originally depicted the king of Poland trampling a Turkish soldier underfoot. Unfortunately, the Poles refused to accept the monument, so the sculptor found himself stuck with a large and unusual statue. Undaunted, he made some minor changes in the statue and succeeded in selling it to the British. However, he neglected to change one detail: Cromwell is wearing a turban.

They Knew What They Liked

The Dutch Civic Guard, which commissioned Rembrandt's world-famous painting "Night Watch," was deeply disappointed with the painting.

♦ ♦ ♦ ♦ ♦

The *Mona Lisa* is undoubtedly the most famous and most valuable painting in the world. However, the husband of the woman depicted in the *Mona Lisa* is said to have disliked the painting so much that he refused to pay for it. It once hung in the bathroom of Francis I, the King of France.

There were several queens of Egypt named Cleopatra but *none* of them was Egyptian. They were all members of a royal family that came from Macedonia, an ancient kingdom located in the region of modern-day Greece. An interesting sidelight is that she (and all other female Egyptian leaders) always wore a stylized fake beard when presiding over court functions.

◆ ◆ ◆ ◆ ◆

Every thoroughbred racehorse in the world has a blood line that can be traced back to one of three Arabian stallions imported into England in the 1700's. The horses were named Darley Arabian, Godolphin Barb and Byerly Turk.

◆ ◆ ◆ ◆ ◆

The Russians have falsely claimed credit for such inventions as the automobile, the telephone, and television. However, one invention that they really did create was the roller coaster. The first ones appeared in the 17th century and were called "Russian Mountains." They consisted of a steep undulating course and small sleds without wheels. Obviously, the course could only be used in the wintertime.

The French were the first to create a roller coaster with wheels. It was introduced in 1804.

Although roller coasters are thought of as amusement rides, the first roller coaster in the U.S. was used in industry. It was an inclined railway that carried hoppers of coal from a mine near Mauch Chunk, Pennsylvania. The track was designed with inclines and drops so that the cars wouldn't gain too much speed.

The first real roller coaster in the U.S. was introduced at Coney Island in 1884.

◆ ◆ ◆ ◆ ◆

There's a superstition among theatre people, especially British actors, that peacock feathers on stage or references to peacocks will bring bad luck.

Nevertheless, when color television was introduced in the U.S., the National Broadcasting Company chose a peacock as its corporate symbol. It didn't seem to bring any bad luck to the network during the following years. In 1975, however, business was bad and the network decided to replace the peacock with a new symbol. After hiring research consultants, outside design firms and printers at a cost of over $750,000, the company unveiled its new symbol: a simple stylized "N."

No sooner had the peacock been retired than the network was hit with the threat of a lawsuit from a tiny educational television station in Nebraska. The little Nebraska station had registered a new symbol that was virtually identical to NBC's. There was one important difference, however: whereas NBC had spent $750,000 on the research, design and printing of its new symbol, the little Nebraska station had come up with the same symbol for the total cost of about $120. On the day the lawsuit was settled, an NBC executive claimed that he heard the peacock mutter "Gotcha!"

◆   ◆   ◆   ◆   ◆

People who own large or ferocious dogs often post a "Beware of the dog" notice so that visitors won't get bitten. The ancient Romans used to post the exact same sign outside their homes (In Latin, "Beware of the dog" is "Cave canem") but they did it for an entirely different reason.

Many Romans owned tiny Italian greyhounds that often weighed as little as six pounds. Because the dogs were so small, people occasionally stepped on them. So the Romans put up signs saying "Beware of the dog," not to protect visitors from being bitten but to protect their dogs from being stepped on.

◆   ◆   ◆   ◆   ◆

Ernest Hemingway rewrote the ending of *A Farewell to Arms* no less than 39 times before he was finally satisfied with it.

◆   ◆   ◆   ◆   ◆

The song "Loch Lomond" tells the story of two Scottish soldiers imprisoned by the British at Carlisle Castle in 1745. One is set free, one is executed. The condemned man will return home via the low road of death and reach Loch Lomond before his friend, who must travel the earthly high road.

◆   ◆   ◆   ◆   ◆

In a conversation between George M. Cohan and a veteran who had fought at the Battle of Gettysburg during the Civil War, the veteran pointed to the American flag and commented, "She's a grand old rag." Cohan was struck by the phrase, and wrote a song entitled "You're a Grand Old Rag." Patriotic groups were outraged and barraged him with complaints over his references to the American flag as a "rag." Cohan promptly changed the title, and the song is now the famous patriotic song, "You're a Grand Old Flag."

◆   ◆   ◆   ◆   ◆

In the popular song, "Pop Goes the Weasel," the word "pop" is British slang meaning "to pawn something." The term "weasel" refers to the tools of one's trade. The phrase "Pop Goes the Weasel" therefore means you are so broke that you have to pawn the means of your livelihood.

◆   ◆   ◆   ◆   ◆

The models for Grant Wood's famous painting, "American Gothic," were his sister wearing a high-necked dress and the family dentist holding a pitchfork, in a pose of prim, hard-nosed morality. It was later discovered that the house in the background that gives the painting its name was actually a bordello.

◆   ◆   ◆   ◆   ◆

◆18◆
UNHAPPY ENDINGS

In 1428, the fourth Earl of Salisbury became the first man to use the cannon in battle. Unfortunately, he also became the first person to be killed by a cannon.

◆　◆　◆　◆　◆

There is a statue in London dedicated to the memory of the first man to be run over by a railroad train. The victim was William Huskisson, a popular member of Parliament who was noted for having a "peculiar aptitude for accident." The bumbling old gentleman entered the record books as the first man to be run over by a railroad train on September 15, 1830, at the opening ceremonies of the Manchester to Liverpool Railroad, when he spotted the Duke of Wellington standing on the other side of the tracks and rushed over to speak to him, neglecting to look both ways before he crossed the tracks.

The bereaved public erected a memorial in Pimlico Gardens consisting of an eight-foot marble statue of Huskisson clad in a Roman toga.

◆ ◆ ◆ ◆ ◆

Beau Brummel, the prototype of an English man of fashion, lost his place in high society, was imprisoned for debt and died a slovenly pauper in a charitable asylum in 1840.

◆ ◆ ◆ ◆ ◆

A house where Thomas Jefferson was said to have written part of the American Declaration of Independence was torn down in the early 1970's to make way for a hamburger stand.

◆ ◆ ◆ ◆ ◆

The career of Balboa, the great explorer who discovered the Pacific Ocean, came to an untimely end in 1517 when he was beheaded on trumped-up charges of treason.

◆ ◆ ◆ ◆ ◆

Charles Goodyear, the originator of vulcanized rubber, was in jail for debt when he started his experiments. Although his discoveries earned large sums of money, he died over $200,000 in debt.

◆ ◆ ◆ ◆ ◆

Although he wrote about 120 books, Horatio Alger was virtually penniless during much of his later life. Alger, who wrote moralistic rags-to-riches stories for boys, has often had his memory tarnished by amusing but untrue anecdotes about his life. One story is quite possibly true: at the age of sixty, Alger is said to have become involved in a wild affair with a married woman. The woman's husband found out and took her away to Paris. Financially destitute, Alger wrote the inspirational novels *Frank and Fearless* and *Upward and Onward* in only 27 days, and used the money to pursue the woman to Paris, where she rejected him. Alger supposedly had a nervous breakdown and returned to New York, where he took lodging in a rooming house. After his only friend in New York died, he went to live with his sister in Massachusetts, where he died in 1899.

◆ ◆ ◆ ◆ ◆

American novelist Stephen Crane was unable to find a publisher willing to publish his first book, *Maggie: A Girl of the Streets*, so he borrowed some money to publish it himself under a pseudonym. The paperbound book sold only two copies.

One cold, wintry night, Crane used the pile of remaining unsold copies as fuel in his fireplace.

◆ ◆ ◆ ◆ ◆

The great composer Robert Schumann died in an insane asylum. Schumann is not to be confused with the composer Johann Schobert, who died—along with his entire household—as a result of eating toadstools. Schobert, of course, is not to be confused with Franz Schubert, who died in miserable poverty of typhus at the age of 31.

◆ ◆ ◆ ◆ ◆

Bonnie Prince Charlie, who is the subject of much romantic legend, spent the last forty years of his life as an alcoholic in Rome.

◆ ◆ ◆ ◆ ◆

Stonewall Jackson, one of the greatest Confederate generals during the American Civil War, was accidentally shot to death by his own troops during the Battle of Chancellorsville.

♦   ♦   ♦   ♦   ♦

The Cavern Club, the legendary Liverpool nightclub and rock music shrine where the Beatles made their start, was torn down to make way for a suburban railway line.

♦   ♦   ♦   ♦   ♦

Robespierre, who urged the application of swift harsh measures under the Reign of Terror during the French Revolution, was himself summarily tried and executed in 1794.

♦   ♦   ♦   ♦   ♦

The Irish-born beauty Lola Montez became a baroness and countess and was the mistress of Bavaria's Ludwig the First. At the height of her popularity, she virtually controlled the government of Bavaria. Later, deported from the country, she studied dancing and became the sweetheart of the American Wild West. She devoted her later years to helping "fallen women" in New York City. She died in poverty in 1861.

♦   ♦   ♦   ♦   ♦

The great French playwright, Moliere, was playing the lead role of the hypochondriac in his own satirical play, *The Imaginary Invalid*, when he was stricken and died.

♦   ♦   ♦   ♦   ♦

The Colossus of Rhodes, one of the greatest of the Seven Wonders of the World, was carted away by Arab invaders in 653 and the bronze was sold as scrap.

♦   ♦   ♦   ♦   ♦

When cowboy star Roy Rogers' horse, Trigger, died, Rogers had him stuffed, mounted and put on display at the Roy Rogers Museum in California. Bullet, the dog beloved by millions of television watchers, joined Trigger on display at the museum several years later.

◆ ◆ ◆ ◆ ◆

The Empress Carlotta, wife of Emperor Maximilian of Mexico, became an archduchess at the age of seventeen and an empress when she was only twenty-three. Shortly thereafter, she became insane and spent the next sixty years of her life as a madwoman until her death in 1927.

◆ ◆ ◆ ◆ ◆

Lorenzo da Ponte, who wrote the librettos for the Mozart operas *Don Giovanni*, *The Marriage of Figaro*, and *Cosi Fan Tutte*, emigrated to the United States in the early 1800s and operated a grocery store in Elizabeth, New Jersey.

◆ ◆ ◆ ◆ ◆

Jason, the legendary leader of the Argonauts, who survived wars, storms, and monsters, died when the prow of his ship, the "Argo," toppled over on him.

◆ ◆ ◆ ◆ ◆

Josef V. D. Stalin, during whose reign an estimated 30,000,000 people were murdered or starved to death, was a theology student in his youth.

◆ ◆ ◆ ◆ ◆

THE ONE AND ONLY

By the year 2005, the largest man-made pyramid in the world will be located in New York City.

For over 4,500 years the Great Pyramid of Cheops in Egypt has held the record as the world's largest pyramid. Its original height was 481 feet and it has now eroded to 450 feet.

However, New York City is currently working on a huge public works project to construct a 505-foot-tall pyramid made of garbage at Fresh Kills on Staten Island. It will rival even the creations of nature and will be the tallest mountain on the Atlantic coast between Florida and a cluster of higher mountains in Maine. It will be 200 feet taller than the nearby Statue of Liberty.

When finished, officials say, the pyramid will be "attractively landscaped."

◆ ◆ ◆ ◆ ◆

If you took all the stones from the huge pyramid of Cheops in Egypt, you could build a ten-foot-high wall around France.

◆ ◆ ◆ ◆ ◆

The spire of the Chrysler Building is one of the most famous landmarks in New York. The interesting thing is that the builders tricked their rivals into thinking that the building was going to be considerably shorter, without any spire at all.

Walter Chrysler wanted to have the honor and prestige of having the tallest building in the world. The problem was that The Bank of Manhattan had announced the construction of a building at 40 Wall Street that was going to claim the honor of "World's tallest building." Chrysler feared that if he revealed his true plans for the Chrysler Building, he would get into an expensive contest with his rival, with each of them tacking on extra height, one story at a time, to gain the one and only distinction.

The building of the spire was treated as a top-secret project. The parts were brought to the site and secretly assembled within the top stories of the building. Without its spire, the Chrysler Building was 871 feet tall, exactly 50 feet shorter than its Wall Street rival.

Then, as the building neared completion in the fall of 1929, Chrysler played his trump card, jacking the entire 175-foot spire up out of its hiding place. In a matter of hours, the Chrysler Building was indisputably the "World's tallest building." Ironically enough, it held the title only briefly before being overshadowed by the Empire State Building.

◆ ◆ ◆ ◆ ◆

St. Patrick's Cathedral in New York was designed by an Episcopalian.

◆ ◆ ◆ ◆ ◆

Hawaii—the only American state that was once an independent kingdom ruled by a royal family.

◆ ◆ ◆ ◆ ◆

Kiwi—the only bird with nostrils at the end of its bill.

◆ ◆ ◆ ◆ ◆

Mercury—the only metal that exists as a liquid at ordinary temperatures.

◆ ◆ ◆ ◆ ◆

Grover Cleveland—the only President who was married in a ceremony held in the White House.

◆ ◆ ◆ ◆ ◆

Andrew Johnson—the only President who later became a senator.

◆ ◆ ◆ ◆ ◆

William Howard Taft—the only President to later serve as Chief Justice of the Supreme Court.

◆ ◆ ◆ ◆ ◆

Louisiana—the only state with counties called "parishes."

◆ ◆ ◆ ◆ ◆

St. John the Evangelist—the only one of the twelve apostles to die a natural death.

◆   ◆   ◆   ◆   ◆

Lake Michigan—the only one of the Great Lakes that lies entirely within the United States.

◆   ◆   ◆   ◆   ◆

Libra—the only zodiac sign represented by an inanimate object.

◆   ◆   ◆   ◆   ◆

Massachusetts—the only one of the 13 original colonies that is still governed by its original constitution.

◆   ◆   ◆   ◆   ◆

Nepal—the world's only Hindu kingdom.

◆   ◆   ◆   ◆   ◆

Eleanor of Aquitaine—the only woman to have been married to both the King of France and the King of England.

◆   ◆   ◆   ◆   ◆

Louisiana—the only state whose legal system is not based upon the common law of England. (It is based on the Napoleonic Code.)

◆   ◆   ◆   ◆   ◆

Thailand—the only Southeast Asian nation that has never been a colony of another nation.

◆   ◆   ◆   ◆   ◆

Sea horse—the only fish with a grasping tail.

◆   ◆   ◆   ◆   ◆

Hawaii—the only state whose borders are entirely naturally defined.

♦   ♦   ♦   ♦   ♦

Bee—the only insect that produces food that is eaten by man.

♦   ♦   ♦   ♦   ♦

Charles I—the only English king to be beheaded.

♦   ♦   ♦   ♦   ♦

Yes, it's true. The original Marlboro man died of emphysema. His name was David Millar. No comment is necessary.

♦   ♦   ♦   ♦   ♦

In 1943, the U.S. Marine Corps awarded a Purple Heart to a Jeep "wounded" in the titanic battle at Guadalcanal in the South Pacific.

♦   ♦   ♦   ♦   ♦

The original "Real McCoy" wasn't a real McCoy.

In 1891, an Indiana farmboy named Norman Selby embarked on a phenomenally successful career as a prizefighter, using the name "Kid McCoy." Year after year, he fought at least one major fight a month, winning most by knockout.

Boxing promoters tried to cash in on his fame with a host of imitation Kid McCoys. Any confusion about who was the "real" McCoy ended on March 24, 1899, when The Kid, in a bloody and grueling bout that cost him three broken ribs, finished off the legendary Joe Choynski in the 20th round.

The *San Francisco Examiner's* boxing writer proclaimed, "NOW YOU'VE SEEN THE REAL MCCOY!"

♦   ♦   ♦   ♦   ♦

ABOUT THE AUTHOR

Paul Stirling Hagerman has been the editorial supervisor and writer of quiz programs for the BBC in London and for all three major American networks, as well as being a contributor to many other television projects in Europe and Australia.

Collaborating with Academy Award–winning filmmaker Robin Lehman, he's added his quirky vision to such documentary films as *Manimals* and *Forever Young*, which have garnered a total of over 35 major awards at international film festivals.

As editor-in-chief, Mr. Hagerman supervised two dozen of the nation's top trivia experts and also dipped into his own vast files of off-beat information to create the best-selling trivia board game, "Stage Two".

He was also a major contributor to the best-selling *The Book of Lists*, and considers his compilation of "15 Famous Historical Events That Occurred in the Bathtub" to be one of the crowning achievements of his career.

INDEX